3/14

Joseph,

This is A gift from
your Mother. May this
book open your life
to success in life

They are Unlimited !!

WHAT PEOPLE ARE SAYING ABOUT DR. MICHAEL GROSS AND *THE SPIRITUAL PRIMER*

"This *Spiritual Primer* contains many universal laws and spiritual principles to assist readers in enriching their lives when applied. Read with caution; it may change your life for the better."

— Michael B. Beckwith Founder, Agape International Spiritual Center, Author of *Spiritual Liberation & Life Vision*

"Being Dr. Michael Gross's close personal friend, I can truly testify to the depth of his deep spiritual wisdom, kind and generous heart, high integrity, and unending dedication to the service of humanity. *The Spiritual Primer* is full of his profound wisdom, awakening readers to their own innate divinity and giving guidance to every area of their lives. I highly recommend this brilliant book to one and all on their journeys of self-discovery and search for universal truth."

— Alisha Killebrew, Clairvoyant Channel, Spiritual Medium, Healer, and Minister

"Michael Gross's *The Spiritual Primer* is the book the world has been waiting for. Now we can all learn not only how to create our own destinies but how to achieve them faster and in a humane way that helps each of us to heal our body, mind, and soul while also healing the planet."

— Patrick Snow, Best-Selling Author of *Creating Your Own Destiny* and *Boy Entrepreneur*

"Michael Gross performed a healing on me in 1999. I was in the hospital recuperating from myocarditis and had lost my eyesight. After I had been blind for five days, the doctors told my family I would never see again. Then my daughter brought Michael to the hospital to do a healing on me late one evening. I woke up the next day and could see again! My doctor said, "It was a miracle." I believe Michael has a special healing power, and I am lucky he came to see me. Still working and enjoying life after all these years. Thank you, Michael."

— Lynn Henderson, Burien, WA

"I worked with Michael Gross for two years. He helped me bolster the putty that joined the islands of self, cementing them with love that slowly became confidence. Even after I moved, he was only a phone call away for me. Every life he touches shines brighter and his words of light going out into the world give us hope for civilization. If only a fraction of people follow the examples he shares in this book and wake up and shine their lights, the world will be better for it."

— Sharon Ingersoll, San Francisco, CA

"For the past twenty-six years, I have had the pleasure and honor of knowing Dr. Michael Gross. In 1991, I joined a class that Michael was teaching on self-empowerment in Kent, Washington. It was obvious to me from the very beginning that Michael was the missing ingredient in my life. It is said that when the student is ready, the teacher will come. As the years continue to pass, I learn many wonderful lessons from Michael and continue to do that to this very day. Michael has a magical energy about him that captures your heart and brings happiness into any space he enters. His level of spiritual enlightenment far surpasses many of the popular teachers today. I highly recommend Michael's new book *The Spiritual Primer* and cannot wait to soak in the knowledge that he has put forth for all of us to utilize in our own personal spiritual adventures. Bless you, Michael."

— Vicki Hanna, Student and Forever Friend

"Dr. Michael Gross, a.k.a. my father from a past life, is one of the most spiritually connected individuals and teachers I have ever met. His teachings connected me to the Source of all Sources (The True Source) and his new book, *The Spiritual Primer*, will take you to the secret of happiness. I have learned the meaning of self-love, and in return, I can change the patterns for three generations forward. I am truly blessed to have crossed paths with this incredible and spiritually connected man. You are truly blessed to pick up this book, let alone read it."

— **Nastaran Cohen, Encino, CA**

"I've had the pleasure to know Dr. Michael Gross for over twenty-two years. I have been his student, he officiated at my son's wedding, and he did a special remarriage ceremony for my husband and me. When a lump was discovered in my right breast, he helped me heal, through the power of God, the True Source, and after four sessions, the lump was gone, which an ultrasound later confirmed. Never doubt the healing power of God, the True Source, of which we are all part. As Michael teaches, if you do the work of the True Source, all your needs will be taken care of. It may not be the way you think it should be, but it will be perfect in every way."

— **Sandra Whiting, RN**

"I've been one of Michael students for fifteen years. I practice his spiritual teachings daily. He has changed my life for the better. I am very grateful to know him."

— **Cathie Nelson, City, Lacy, WA**

"*The Spiritual Primer* is not just another self-help or spirituality book. It's not for the faint-hearted but those who truly want to learn more about the universe and how it operates and why that is intensely relevant to the daily lives of each and every one of us."

— **Larry Alexander, MA and Co-Owner of
Superior Book Productions**

"Michael, thank you for the love and knowledge you share. It has helped me grow spiritually beyond measure. I've been able to see myself in a different way and to experience more happiness and joy in my life. Things that once seemed insignificant have taken on new meaning. The world is a brighter place with you as our spiritual teacher and mentor."

— Michelle Wealther, RN, Reiki Practitioner, and Certified Nutritional Advisor at Sanoviv Medical Institute

"I loved reading *The Spiritual Primer*. It finally made me understand karma and karmic debt in an easy-to-understand way. There is so much information to chew on here, to ingest and allow to course through your body to rejuvenate you. Before you are done, you'll be ready to fulfill your life mission—don't believe you have one? Read this book and you'll learn differently."

— Tyler R. Tichelaar, PhD and Award-Winning Author of *Spirit of the North: A Paranormal Romance* and *The Children of Arthur* Series

"What a comfort it was to discover that I have so much more control in my life than I had ever thought possible before reading this book."

— Barbara Todd, Spanaway, WA

"I felt a strong connection when I was referred to Michael in 1999 by another spiritual teacher. After a series of individual sessions, I enrolled as a student in his empowerment training class series. As my teacher and counselor over the years, he's provided me with guidance and tools to help me navigate through day-to-day life with more grace and confidence. He's done the same for many others, often going above and beyond to 0encourage and assist his clients and friends."

— Janine Marie Redman, Puyullup, WA

"By the time I met Dr. Michael Gross, I had realized something (Divine Providence, guardian angels, the hand of God, something more than just luck alone) was intervening at just the right time to keep me healthy and alive. During the first meeting, Dr. Michael Gross's first words confirmed what I had realized. Had Michael said anything else, I would've seriously doubted that he was the next step in a journey that began with my becoming a Reiki master. While attending Dr. Michael Gross's classes, I began noticing changes in my interactions with others in the workplace; I was more readily accepted, my presence enjoyed and even appreciated. I have found a home in Dr. Michael Gross's classes and now see myself continuing my journey and changing and growing."

— **Michael Fort, Lakewood, WA**

"A helpful guide to those seeking answers to navigating life."

— **Denise Clark, Whidbey Island, WA**

"Dr. Michael Gross's book *The Spiritual Primer* is a priceless gift! It provides one's spirit the necessary support and understanding to identify what changes need to be made to live a more authentic, connected, and aware existence. Pick up this book, reconnect with God, The True Source, and be ready to expand your heart and discover how to tap into life's blessings!"

— **Vanessa Valencia, Author of *Mamma's Planet Earth***

"Michael Gross has proven to be an amazing resource in my life. Kind, intelligent, and totally tuned into the spiritual realm, Michael has offered insightful, succinct feedback on my life's most pressing issues. His wisdom coupled with his generous heart is a powerful combination providing spot-on guidance."

— **Lucky McCullough, Maui Life Coach**

"Dr. Michael Gross has a wealth of experience in guiding his clients to connect with God's true nature so they can achieve their fullest potentials. Be it healing those in need, training students on spiritual practices, or sharing his amazing intuitive gifts, Michael's varied and rich background has allowed him to formulate twelve spiritual laws invaluable to anyone seeking deeper meaning and a strengthened capacity to succeed. So no matter what your spiritual or philosophical beliefs, Michael's twelve spiritual laws are a straightforward, usable, and potent toolbox for everyday life challenges and the enrichment of the soul."

— Bill Yarborough

"*The Spiritual Primer* is all about creating a life of unlimited joy, happiness, prosperity, and fulfillment. This book is a must-read because it will change your life, positively, forever."

— Eric Lofholm

"I am thrilled Dr. Michael Gross wrote this helpful and inspiring book. This book will guide you and support you through your most difficult moments and encourages you to keep going no matter what. Whenever you feel at a loss and need balance and energy, pick up Michael's book and enjoy the strength it gives you! Thank you Dr. Michael Gross for all you do and writing this book!"

— Karina Taugwalder, Author and Owner of Online Presence Care

"Dr. Michael takes a topic that has been debated for decades—religion vs. spirituality—and breaks it down into logical steps. Religion and spirituality do indeed go hand in hand and embracing this realization has taken my personal spiritual practice to a new, simplified and more fulfilling level."

— Jen Melle, Lynwood, WA

"This book, written through the insight of Dr. Michael Gross, has ultimately reassured me of the existence of spirituality and the natural laws of nature that exist. One might call spirituality one's inner voice, or trusting your gut for the right decision, or even an aspect of karma. We all have at one time in our lives searched for something greater, something bigger than ourselves and a source of answers, when we find ourselves lost in doubt and second guess our thoughts and behaviors. This book has truly enlightened me that no matter what side of life we find ourselves on, call it the good or the bad, yin and yang, that there is always balance in the universe, and that balance is kept in check through natural unexplainable laws of nature. I find it ironic that throughout the world, when there is grief, tragedy, and an outpouring of misery, that with time there always seems to be a light at the end of the dark tunnel. This book brings that mysterious light into perspective; it opens our minds that there are natural laws that the universe works in, that guide our way into tomorrow. These laws of the universe are expressed here; together they work and create that light at the end of the tunnel, giving one hope for a brighter future and illuminating our path along the way. Even as the light of a dimly lit candle chases away the darkness so that we can see our way, so too are these spiritual natural laws. Working together, they brighten our light not only to illuminate our path in life but to brighten and warm our souls as the sun does on a warm summer's day. I recommend this book to anyone who wants to see his or her path again, to chase the darkness from the soul, and all of the feelings that come with it. When you learn how to work with the natural laws of the spirit, your life will be so much warmer and brighter, and not only will they light the path before you, but they will allow you to light the world around yourself, guiding you and everyone around you, as you apply them to your life. Thank you, Dr. Gross, for your insight into the world we live in and the laws of spirituality that make our lives a little brighter. I know, through applying what I have learned in your book, I can see my life in a whole new light, and I will never get lost in the darkness again."

— Dean Paulson

"Knowing Dr. Gross for over sixty years, I can attest to his knowledge and understanding of life and its spiritualities. This book is a fantastic guideline to anyone wanting to understand spirituality and how to apply it to our lives. It explains how to achieve prosperity, happiness, health, and abundance. A road map to true enlightenment.

— Alan A. Sloane

"Michael Gross's book is the best way to learn how to not only heal our body, mind and soul, but also how we can grow ourselves in a way that also heals the planet. This book is necessary for all of us to ascend as well as complete our missions and goals."

– Alisa Muller

"As a survivor of domestic violence, I struggled in a life of limited beliefs. I was grateful to be building my life away from abuse, but I felt there was something missing. When I met Dr. Michael Gross, I was thrilled to receive my copy of *The Spiritual Primer*. In that first meeting, I experienced my soul awakening! It is the missing piece I had been seeking! Dr. Michael has become my dearest friend, my spiritual coach and partner on many projects. I am eternally grateful he is in my life. Truly, a humble man with insurmountable wisdom, who is the epitome of integrity, honesty, and a visionary on a mission to bring unconditional love to the world."

— Tiiu Napp, Author of *Healing the Holes in Your Soul*

APPLYING GOD'S TWELVE TRANSFORMATIONAL LAWS TO REAWAKEN YOUR SOUL

THE
SPIRITUAL
PRIMER

RECONNECTING TO GOD TO
EXPERIENCE YOUR TRUE SOURCE'S
LOVE, JOY, AND HAPPINESS

AVIVA
PUBLISHING

DR. MICHAEL GROSS

DEDICATION

To my beautiful, compassionate loving mother, Mildred Silverman Gross (1915-1968), who resides in the bosom of God, The True Source: you were and are a great inspiration in everything I do in my life. I have not forgotten your words, your support, your enthusiasm, your compassion and unconditional love. You are my greatest gift. Because of your faith and belief in me, I dedicate this book to you. Thank you, Mom, for all of your love and support.

To my beloved sister, Francine Rubman (1938-2021), thank you for being there for me and believing in me.

To my son, Seth, whom I referred to when he was young, with the metaphor "my captain." You have turned out to become a rock and leader in your life and community. I believe the quote by David Bly, "Your children will become what you are; so be what you want them to be," applies to both you and your beautiful wife, Jessica. You both exemplify this with your children. *Thank you for your support and love.* I am so proud of both of you for what you have accomplished and feel blessed to have such beautiful grandchildren as Fareday, Nora, and Jeep. I know that both of you will inspire your children to great successes in their lives to become not only leaders in their community but successful parents as well.

To my beloved daughter, Heidi, whom I referred to then and now as my beautiful princess, you have always been very special in my life and you continue to be so evermore. I hope this book will inspire you for the many great things to come. To my grandson, Jonah, may this book open the door to greatness and success in your life.

To my surrogate brother, Alan and his wife Gloria Sloane, thank you for your lifelong support in all that I do.

To Rebecca Paulin, thank you for your confidence in reminding me to write this book. I know you are looking down from heaven and smiling and saying "It's about time!"

To my surrogate sister, Alisha Killebrew, thank you for your support, encouragement, undying friendship, and love in helping me to write this book. *You are my rock.*

To Patrick Snow, my adopted son, who is my mentor in assisting me in writing this book. Thank you for your wisdom, confidence, and constant encouragement. Without your assistance, I don't know whether I could have written this book so easily.

To Nastaran Cohen, my daughter from another lifetime, I thank you for your constant support and unconditional love.

Acknowledgments

I would like to thank Tyler Tichelaar for his incredible editing skills. The skills that have helped this book make sense.

To Shiloh Schroeder, Jessi Carpenter, and Rachel Langaker, thank you for your awesome work in laying out my book and your incredible cover design expertise.

Thank you, Sandra Whiting, for your encouragement in writing this book.

Additional thanks to Michael Fort, Cecile Staples, Jim and Mia Perryman, Colby Wilks, Ken Shelton, Sharon Cantor, Barbara Todd, Ilse and Jim Johnson, Kuhn Kahn, George Boozer, Deborah Erickson, Bob Parker, Denise Clark, Helen Cameron, Betty Richardson, Helgy Yngvason, Shannie Yngvason, Jaquy Yngvason, Tom Paulin, Kathy McWilliams, Lori Bullock, Lori Lindros, Marta Castillo, Sharon Manessa, Pete Perkins, Sharon Rose, Barbara Todd, Shirley Smith, Mario del Rosario, Joe Jones, Lynn Henderson, Janine Marie Redman, Denise Clark, Larry Alexander, Vicki Hannah, Vanessa Valencia, Kelly and Bob Parker, Dean Paulson, Laree Neely, Lori Bullock, Michael Beckwith, James Beck, Jason Suess, Karina Taugwalder, Shirleen Reeves, Rev. June Gatlin, Annie Poole, Deborah W. Ellis, Michelle Wealther, Julie Marincovich, Hans and Ingrid Skacel, my nieces Lisa, Allison, Sherryl, and Jamie, my many students, and most of all, to *God, the True Source*.

CONTENTS

Part III: FAQ's, Affirmations, and Manifestations

"You don't know that you don't know.
You know you don't know.
You don't know you know.
You know that you know."

— Old Taoist proverb

FOREWORD

BY PATRICK SNOW

I grew up in a very religious family in Michigan. I had a loving mother and father and was the fourth of five children. My family never missed going to Mass on Sunday, and all of my siblings attended Catholic grade school. My father, one of the greatest men I've ever known and one of the most impactful upon my life, earned his living as a teacher and a coach in the Catholic school system for more than forty years. I had the best parents and siblings that a kid could ask for, and I continue to benefit from the morals, values, and ethics I learned growing up as a "good Catholic boy." But for me, it was more about the sports, and less about the church. For whatever reason—I'm not sure why—I never became a big Notre Dame fan.

Late in high school, I participated in the Fellowship of Christian Athletes club where I learned the importance of developing a personal relationship with Jesus Christ. That relationship has served me well for many years; my faith in Christ has gotten me through some very tough times. After graduating from high school, I headed west to attend the University of Montana where I continued to participate in the local Catholic Church youth group and went on many retreats and also ski trips. It was a fun time. Later at the end of college, I was getting ready to marry my college sweetheart (who was not Catholic). She quickly decided that she was not going to go through the Catholic pre-marriage classes or convert to Catholicism. When I shared this news with the priest whom I wanted to marry us, I was advised that if I married her, I would not be welcome in the Catholic Church any longer. *Wow!* I thought to myself. *I think I have just been kicked out of the church!* I walked away from the Catholic Church that day a free man, thinking that my departure from the Church was a bigger loss for it, than for me. I was happy, and I was a free man!

Over the next twenty-five or so years of my life, I viewed myself as a non-denominational Christian living by "God-made rules," while not always following all the "man-made rules!" I bounced around from church to church, never really finding a place to land. After a while, I just quit going to church altogether, even though my belief and my relationship with Jesus Christ were very strong. I once heard a quote that said, "It is better to be out fishing thinking of God, than to be in church thinking of fishing." This summed me up well. I found my God and faith in nature and in the outdoors. I continued on my Christian path and raised two amazing sons. I created a successful career for myself as a professional speaker, best-selling author, and a publishing coach. Then a devastating blow occurred in my life when I was forty-six.

My father, John "Jack" Thomas Snow was diagnosed with pancreatic cancer at age seventy-three and lost this battle when he passed at age seventy-four on July 28, 2015. My father was my rock, my best friend, my mentor, my coach, and my spiritual advisor. Two of the most important things I learned from him were: "My God is too big for any one religion" and "Family is the most important thing in the world so you need to fight like hell to preserve and protect your family always!"

As a professional speaker living in Hawaii, with my father living in Florida, I was flying way, way too much. Between speaking engagements in New Zealand and multiple trips to see my father back in Florida before he passed, being on an airplane quickly became a very bad experience for me. Sometime before my father's passing, I started suffering from panic attacks on planes. I'd never had any health issues previously, but soon, anxiety, fear, stress, and tension were an everyday normal way of living for me. I was in complete crisis after my father's passing, and I even went to the ER twice thinking I was having a heart attack. Those incidents turned out to be panic attacks, and the doctor prescribed medication to me for them. However, I refused to take the medication because I believed there had to be a natural way to be cured of these ailments.

Then I began to ask myself, *What is the meaning of life? What truly happens after death? Why did my dad have to die at seventy-four when I could have more easily let him go at eighty-four, or for sure, ninety-four?* I also continued to wonder why since his passing I had started picking up other people's feelings, energy, and pain. Soon I did not want to leave home. I could barely work, and I was a complete wreck emotionally, physically, and spiritually.

During my early years, I could not even spell "spirituality," let along know how to define it. Later in my life, I learned the truth from what Deepak Chopra said: "Religion is based on someone else's experiences whereas spirituality is based on your own." Well, something had to give because I was a wreck, and I had apparently been given the gift of being an "empath" as a result of my father's passing. I felt it was a curse, and I just wanted my normal life back. This new life of feeling other people's pain and negative energy combined with years of negativity, tension, and stress building up in my system completely paralyzed me. I could no longer fly. I was fearful of virtually everything (especially death), and I was thinking of retiring from the speaking business. My whole life was turned upside down. All the experts said I was just grieving my father's loss, but in reality, it was so much more. I had learned about energy, especially negative energy, and I had so much negative energy in me that it virtually paralyzed me.

Long story short, I flew to Seattle (although I hated flying because I always worried when the next panic attack would kick in) for a publishing video shoot. At this shoot, I was blessed to meet Dr. Michael Gross, who attended my video shoot. He was eager to learn more about me so he could publish his book he had wanted to write for many years. We quickly hit it off like old friends, and over time, I shared with him all of the challenges I was facing. Later, I learned that we had lived past lives together as friends.

What I discovered from Michael was that often when people experience a huge loss, a spiritual awakening will occur. That was the case for me. What I learned from him quickly was to meditate, release all of this negative energy with love, and let go of the stress, tension, and fear. He taught me how to replace these negative energies with God's unconditional love energy, which is a much stronger energy than fear or negativity. I soon became his student, dialed into all his spirituality calls, invested in his energy healing coaching program, and soaked up every bit of wisdom and knowledge he had to offer. I truly was blessed to find him and his healing coaching.

I quickly learned that Michael's wisdom wasn't learned in books, or from studying with another spiritual guru; it was gifted to him through a connection he had established directly with God and God's unconditional love energy. Michael shared with me that he had established a 24/7 dialogue directly with God. He could ask God any question, on any subject matter, anytime, and God would immediately gift him the knowledge or wisdom needed to answer any and all of these questions. Michael was quick to point out that everyone has this ability, so he is not special. Of course, I was 100 percent skeptical because I was taught that we pray to Jesus, and then Jesus intercedes for us with God, and then maybe we get our prayers answered, and maybe not (depending on whether we are bad or good as a popular Christmas song teaches). But to dialogue and completely communicate back and forth with God—are you kidding me? If this were true, what an amazing discovery—what an amazing gift! Yet I remained very skeptical.

However, in short order in only a few healing sessions, Michael taught me how to meditate, release all of my tension, panic, stress, and anxiety, and to eliminate my fear of flying, my fear of death, my fear of crowds, and my fear of tight spaces. Michael confirmed for me, as I had suspected, that reincarnation is real and that some of our fears (as was the case with me) come into this life's embodiment from our soul wounds in previous lives. Michael then continued to heal me from one ailment after another, and another, and another. Soon, I got my whole life back. I was healed and able to function completely normally again. Not only did Michael assist me in my healing, raise my vibrations, and bring me closer to God, but he also taught me some powerful affirmations that allowed me to manifest a brand-new construction ocean-view home on Maui.

Michael quickly pointed out that he refuses to take credit for any of these healings because he is merely an aspect of God, the True Source, and it was God's unconditional love energy and my open-mindedness to that energy that allowed the healings to occur. But still, I was skeptical until Michael taught me how to connect and communicate with the soul of my late father, Jack Snow.

When Michael told me it was possible to communicate with my father, at first, I didn't believe him. It sounded like the work psychics do when they communicate with the souls of those who have passed over. I missed my father fiercely, and I so wanted to connect with his soul, but was that even possible? Again, I had to keep an open mind. Michael taught me seven steps to go through while meditating in order to connect with my father's soul. He also warned me that it might take twenty or thirty attempts before it would be successful.

Well, later that night, I followed all of the steps Michael had taught me, and it worked perfectly the very first time. In no time, I was connecting and communicating directly with the soul of my father. He was in heaven, and without pain. He was with his mother and father (my grandparents), and he even allowed me to talk with them via this soul connection. I heard their voices and saw their mannerisms as well. At the end of this one-hour session, I was still in disbelief until it came time to say goodbye to my dad. And when I did, he reached down and kissed me right on the lips. I felt the wetness of his lips on my mouth, and it brought me to tears because it was then I knew this experience was real. See, whenever I would fly home to see my dad, he would always meet me in the airport and greet with me with a big hug and a kiss directly on the lips. And, of course, I was always embarrassed, preferring a "man hug." He would say, "You are my son always, and as your dad, I will always kiss you on the lips whenever I greet you!" During this soul-connection session, because my dad finished our time together with the familiar kiss on the lips, I knew it was real. Since then, now my dad's spirit and I can connect 24/7/365, and it only take 3-5 seconds to draw his soul into conversation with me.

But still, I was skeptical. And so I asked myself, *Who is this Dr. Michael Gross? Is he the real deal? Why does he not take credit for these amazing healings? Does he really dialogue with God 24/7/365? Does his connection really allow him to get answers to all of life's most challenging questions?* Even though Michael had completely healed me, I still questioned it. And yet Michael is quick to point out that he did not heal me; rather, it was God working through him to heal me. As you read this book, you will find out that Michael is very, very humble, and he takes credit for none of this. So one night in a meditation/soul-connection session with my father (I don't even know what to call it; I just know it is real), I asked my father whether this Dr. Michael Gross was the real deal, and whether he really does have the ability to have God speak to him and through him to answer all of my questions, your questions, and anyone else's questions who seeks out his counsel?

To my soul, mind, and ears, I clearly heard my father, Jack Snow, say to me from heaven that when he died, he knew how much his passing would have a negative impact upon my entire being. He went on to say that he had brought Michael Gross into my life at seventy-four years of age (the exact same age my father was when he passed) to heal me, guide me, and reconnect my soul to God. There was no question about it. But my father went on to say that he is also quick to give me advice directly by putting his words of advice into Michael's voice so he can also help me navigate through tough times. With this message from my father, I no longer question anything that Michael teaches, and I now 100 percent believe that God is speaking directly to me and to Michael's clients through his voice. Not only have I come to learn and now believe that God wants to have a direct dialogue with me, but I also know he wants to have one with you and with all of his children. What an amazing thing to consider! And as a bonus, I have adopted Dr. Michael Gross as my new dad. I figured now that I was dad-less, perhaps Michael could fill my father's shoes, and he has certainly done so, completely healing me.

But wait—what about my upbringing as a Christian? How does what I've learned from Michael fit with the Christian model of praying to Jesus in order to get to God? What I have come to believe is that just like we are born to both a mother and a father, it is okay to have both a connection with Jesus and a connection directly with God. In fact, two is better than one. As a result, I now view Jesus Christ as my mother figure whom I can pray to at any time, and God as my father figure, whom I can also pray to or communicate with at any time. Furthermore, I have learned that absolutely nothing Michael teaches goes against the Christian faith—nothing! Well, except the reincarnation part. But in my research on this topic, I have learned that even the Bible taught and accepted reincarnation as the truth until 553 AD when the Emperor Justinian manipulated Church doctrine at the Fifth Ecumenical Council to remove all belief in the pre-existence of souls. All references to reincarnation were also omitted from the Bible, except one that was forgotten: "But I tell you, Elijah has come." (Mark 9:13). In this verse, Jesus is referring to John the Baptist as the reincarnation of the Prophet Elijah.

I admit this is a lot of background on me for the foreword to another author's book, but I wanted to write my testimonial here so you can learn firsthand that if a very solid Christian man can learn about other spiritual truths and apply them to his life to heal, then so can you! Michael can provide answers to some of your most anxiety-ridden questions so you can heal and have deeper understanding and a more fruitful life. However, I must say that all of this stuff will only work if you keep an open mind, an open heart, and a healthy curiosity to learn all the things that the religions of the world have failed to teach.

In this powerful book, *The Spiritual Primer*, Dr. Michael Gross will teach you how to reconnect with God's unconditional love energy—the energy that your soul yearns for because it experienced it prior to your embodiment in human form. You will learn to find peace, love, joy, harmony, and bliss. You will learn how to overcome negative energy, defeat tension, remove stress, cure panic attacks, and heal emotionally, physically, and spiritually. You will learn about your "family level missions and goals" as well as your "soul level missions and goals." You will learn about disease, about relationships, about forgiveness, and most importantly, about love. You will learn how to cure all your phobias. You will be able once and for all to know about all those things in life that religion has not been able to answer for you during all of your years of searching.

When you follow the formulas and strategies in this book, you will discover peace of mind, harmony, bliss, and love. Additionally, you will learn how to heal yourself, harnessing the power of God's unconditional love energy. You will learn that it is okay to ask God for anything your soul desires, and you will learn how to achieve it on God's timing through "right action" and "correct exchange."

You will learn how to acquire specific knowledge to heal soul wounds from previous lives, how to create good karma, and how to release karmic debt from past lives. You will learn how to communicate with your loved ones who have passed over to the other side, and you will gain insight and advice from them to live an even better life.

Throughout this book, you will learn that Dr. Michael Gross is *not* about ego or trying to take credit for any of this knowledge! You will learn that all of his material, wisdom, energy healing, and connection comes directly from God. Mostly, you will learn that God is eager to connect directly to you. Once you feel God's unconditional love energy burning in your bones and skin (almost like being in a tanning booth), you will no longer doubt this connection, and you will also be empowered to do the work of God on earth by giving your love and healing energy to a world that now, more than ever, is in need of massive amounts of healing.

Finally, in this book you will learn your life's purpose, and how to act on that purpose to give love and healing to all those in your life—both people you know and those you don't. If every human being on earth were to read this book and be filled with God's unconditional love, there would be no wars, no famine, no fear-mongering, no pain, no injustice, and no unknowingness.

In this book, you will learn that God wants you to join its team and do God's work. (You will learn that God is not male nor female but a gender-neutral energy of pure love; hence, the reason I did not say "his!") My hope for you is that you keep an open mind to everything Michael has written and then open your soul to allow it to sink in. When you do, your life will be forever healed and forever changed, and "Team God" will have won another soul to use as a healing vehicle to spread more love on earth!

If this skeptic can become enlightened to the truth about God and spirituality, so can you! Thank you, God, for allowing Dr. Michael Gross to teach me the power of your unconditional love and for allowing this book to get into print for the benefit of millions of readers for decades to come. Thank you, Dad (Jack Snow), for bringing Dr. Michael Gross into my life, completely introducing me to the power of God's healing energies, and allowing me to adopt him as my new dad to replace you!

Not only are you going to learn all of the things I talked about above, but you are going to learn much, much, much more! The information I have shared in this foreword is just the tip of the iceberg of the wisdom and knowledge you will soon be blessed with. So get ready for an amazing ride! Your life is about to change forever! You will soon experience more love, joy, harmony, and peace, all of which will better serve your soul and humanity at the same time!

I challenge you to open your mind, heart, and soul, and get ready for a heavy dose of God's unconditional love. By doing so, you will finally achieve the peace, love, and joy that you have spent an entire life pursuing. Your search is over. Congratulations. All of your questions about life will be answered in the following pages….

Respectfully,

Patrick Snow

Patrick Snow
International Best-Selling Author of *Creating Your Own Destiny*, *The Affluent Entrepreneur*, and *Boy Entrepreneur*

www.PatrickSnow.com
www.BecomingABestSellingAuthor.com

PREFACE

WHAT IS SPIRITUALITY?

"Religion is belief in someone else's experience. Spirituality is having your own experience. Atheism is no experience only measurement."

— **Deepak Chopra**

Spirituality has often been misunderstood and misaligned. Most religious people believe that spirituality contradicts their own religious beliefs. In fact, this could not be further from the truth. Spirituality enhances religious beliefs. There are certain immutable laws that occur in the universe that are also part of religious beliefs; sometimes, they are defined using different words, but their intent is the same.

The Judeo-Christian, Buddhist, Hindu, etc. belief systems are based on certain spiritual laws, for example: the Ten Commandments or their equivalent. These laws embrace spirituality as well as religious beliefs.

If you can understand that many of our religious beliefs are based in spirituality, then you will understand that the two are intertwined, and when applied properly, they help create your life. Another example is the Law of Karma (what goes around, comes around), the Law of Unconditional Love, the Law of Do Unto Others as You Would Have Them Do Unto You, and many others. By embracing spirituality and realizing that religions are based in spirituality, you can fully understand that the two go hand-in-hand. One commonly held spiritual belief is that you are an aspect of God, the True Source. One only needs to look in the Bible to see the parallel to that spiritual law is "God created mankind in his image; in the image of God he created them; male and female he created them" (Genesis 1:27). Many parallels exist in all religions that embody spiritual beliefs. My only goal in having you read this is for you to realize that the two, religiosity and spiritual belief, are usually in alignment with one another.

Perhaps the best way this can be summed up is with a quote from the Lama, "I believe deeply that we must find, all of us together, a new spirituality. This new concept ought to be elaborated alongside the religions in such a way that all people of goodwill can adhere to it."

INTRODUCTION

MAKING SENSE OF YOUR PURPOSE

"We must be willing to let go of the life we have planned so as to have the life that is waiting for us."

— E. M. Forster

This book is designed to awaken you from your deep slumber to remember who you are and what you are. If you consider yourself a naysayer, doubter, nonbeliever, or atheist, this book was ordained for you. It's okay not to believe its message because I am not trying to change you. I am merely giving you an opportunity to look at life and your origins from a different perspective of reality.

The spiritual laws I will describe in this book for you to employ in your life have nothing to do with religion and more to do with you creating the life you have secretly hoped and desired to achieve. These laws are immutable, reproducible, and apply to all things we do in our lives. You are now faced with a great choice—whether to read this book in its entirety and apply these laws to change your life and all aspects of it or to remain where you are. If you decide to read on, you will now have the opportunity to enjoy life and live it to its fullest! You will find out you are the sole (soul) creator of your life and the opportunities to achieve what you wish to create are unlimited!

If you are satisfied with your life, you do not need to read this book. If you're satisfied with a daily humdrum, ordinary existence, then you do not need to read this book. If all you do is get up and go to work, come home, eat, and go to sleep, and you are satisfied with that lifestyle, you do not need to read this book. If you're not curious about your life, you do not need to read this book. If you are not wondering about what your mission and goal is in life and why you are here, you do not need to read this book. If you think you are nothing but a Social Security number and/or an employee number, you do not need to read this book. If you think you are not important, you do not need to read this book.

But I suspect those descriptions do not fit you. You wouldn't have picked up this book, otherwise. Instead, you're curious about the meaning of life. You wonder why you are here. You wonder what your purpose in life is. You wonder what your missions and goals are. You know there has to be more to life than everyday work. You want to know how to fulfill your dreams. You want to quit feeling stuck, empty, depressed, alone, or abandoned. You want to find more peace and joy in your life.

I once asked the very same questions and wanted the very same things. I would wake up in the night and wonder like you whether this was all there was to life—just eating, sleeping, working, and feeling like a robot. Just like you, I have felt lost and like everything is futile. Just like you, I have felt challenged and wondered where the next dollar would come from, and no matter what I did,

I never felt fulfilled. I would buy items to make myself feel good, and then after I obtained them and the anticipation and thrill of owning them diminished, I found I had to buy more new items and more new items to feel excited again. And then one day, I woke up and asked, "Is there any more to life than what I am experiencing?"

The answer is "Yes!" and in this book, you will learn how to change your life and bring about joy. You'll also learn the history of creation and your part on this planet. You'll find out that you are never alone. You will learn why you're here. You will understand your mission and goal and proceed to achieve it with joy and happiness. You will have the satisfaction of having great success in your life. If you're single, you will attract your perfect mate, and if you are married, you will change your marriage into love and happiness. In this book, you will understand the part you play in the universe and contribute to it wholly. This book will demonstrate and teach you how you can manifest joy, love, abundance, prosperity, and happiness each day of your life. In these pages, you will learn how to create your perfect made-in-heaven miracle mate and even your perfect job. By using the tools in this book, you will achieve your dreams! By reading this book, you will realize that you have had more than one lifetime.

If you open your mind to this book, then you will create the life you have dreamt of and often desired. If you will open your mind to this book, you can create your perfect life. If you apply the techniques I have presented in this book, you'll know what direction to take and never look back. If you will be willing to let go of pre-conceived programming, everything in your life will change. If you allow yourself to be open-minded, then you can achieve great things. If you will not be impatient and instead realize you are creating a new successful path and then you will sit back and observe the miraculous outcome, you will add new vistas to your life. If you realize that life is special and you cherish it, you will achieve great success. You will understand that you are the vehicle that can create anything you so desire in your life. If you practice the techniques I present later in this book, you will change your life…unconditionally!

What I desire is not to change your beliefs, but rather to expand them into new vistas. In this book, you will learn more about your life and more about spirituality than you ever expected. I hope this book will achieve two important things in your life: 1) to answer most, if not all, of your questions about your life, and 2) to inspire you to learn more about spirituality, yourself, and life. Later, I will address how to accomplish this.

Everything and everyone on this planet has asked for life and has received it. What a great and glorious gift we have asked to receive. You see, without our human bodies, we cannot experience the birth of a human life, nor the smell of a fragrant rose, nor feel the warm breeze caressing our bodies, nor see the sunrise and sunset. Nor could we see or feel the joy of our newborn child or see the child grow into adulthood under our tutelage. Life has given us the opportunity to feel human love, to experience human love, to have our heart and body experience love. To receive the gift of life is to have the opportunity to experience all the senses our physical bodies are capable of, unlimitedly! It also gives us the opportunity to learn and heal our karma (life lessons and experiences), both from past lives and current lifetimes. I will also discuss this in more depth in the ensuing chapters.

The knowledge I am imparting to you is the accumulation of over forty-five years of learning, experiencing, remembering my past lives, and being taught by God, the True Source. Every soul who has incarnated on earth or any other planet has several purposes in life. These purposes are on both the human and the spiritual level. I refer to these special purposes as "missions and goals." The missions and goals on the human plane can be broken down to family and life purpose. While family is self-explanatory, life purpose could involve bringing about life-changing inventions or medical breakthroughs, being a leader to bring about positive changes at a micro and macro level, being a mentor to assist someone else in a goal, adopting a child to help him or her reach a goal, etc. There are also spiritual missions and goals, a few of which include helping souls physically, mentally, and emotionally to heal, helping souls incarnate, helping souls cross over to the other side, bringing harmony and balance to this planet or universe, working with nature spirits, or working with Mother Earth. One of my missions and goals is to awaken you from a long slumber of plain old dull existence and into a new life of enlightenment.

The principles presented in this book can be applied to every part of your life, whether it be corporate or personal, career or family or friends, because it creates a roadmap to bring great positive changes and success into every aspect of your life. Just by applying the Twelve Spiritual Laws in this book and the spiritual practices recommended here, all individuals, businesses, and corporations will experience an atmosphere of greater energy, harmony, peace, prosperity, abundance, and joy. After you experience these rewards, people will be clamoring to work for and with you to become part of this total consciousness of enlightenment.

Congratulations! You're about to begin an exciting journey filled with positive experiences and outcomes beyond your wildest imagination. I applaud your verve.

But first, before we jump in with both feet, please take a few minutes to think about what you hope to gain by reading this book. (I encourage you to write your responses because what you learn from reading this book will then become more ingrained in your mind.)

EXERCISE

List below seven dreams you would like to achieve in your life. Don't hold back; the sky's the limit!

_____

_____

_____

_____

_____

_____

_____

I encourage you to use this book as your spiritual primer to reconnect to God to experience your true sources—love, joy, and happiness.

Are you ready to begin? Good, let's get started.

PRELUDE

IN THE BEGINNING

"God has no religion."

— Gandhi

The material you are about to read in this book is not from a common ordinary man who is just speculating about God, The True Source, or reciting (or regurgitating) information about or from previous theological texts or books, because we know there are thousands and thousands of those types of works being published today.

Rather, the contents of this book have been accessed from "The Universal Band of Knowledge" as a result of my speaking directly with God, The True Source, daily for more than forty years, asking questions and receiving huge "downloads" of information into my mind, receiving all of God, The True Source's wisdom in order to make sense of this existence called life that is occurring on planet Earth in our third and fourth dimensional lives. This book also explains why we are here at this time and what our missions and goals are.

The following information centers on what I have learned over the last forty years. This information is now written and shared in this book for your benefit in order for you to grow and to learn who you truly are, why you are here, your origins, and what you can create to have a loving, prosperous, healthy, and joyous life, now, at this very moment! As God, The True Source, always reminds me, all of us, I repeat, all of us are now unlimited! Each and every one of you is now unlimited! So be it!

. . .

Have you ever wondered how all life in the universe began? I have thought about this many, many times, and I will share with you what I have learned. First, let me say that what I am going to describe is an oversimplification. Using the KISS principle (Keep it simple, stupid), I will hopefully help you understand how and why this universe started, your creation, and how you are one with it.

In my youth when I was first learning about religion and God, I thought God was a huge man sitting on a golden throne overlooking the earth and all human beings. I believed that this holy man decreed who would live, who would die, who would be poor, who would be rich, who would marry, who would divorce, who would keep or lose their jobs, who would be punished, who would have a life of pain, who would have a life of fear, who would be sick, who would be healed, etc.

I would now like to share with you what I have learned from God, the True Source. I believe that as you read this book, you will have a better understanding of how the universe was created, why you are here, your connection to the Divine, and more.

I would like you to take a moment to close your eyes and just visualize a vast emptiness with curious little shapes floating around in this nothingness. These curious little shapes are what we call atoms, molecules, atomic and subatomic particles, mitochondria, etc. These shapes appear to be sleeping and drifting in no particular pattern. For the sake of brevity, I have chosen to call all of them "matter." As this matter floats around in what I'll call a dreamland state, it began to develop a sense of itself, and through the Law of Attraction (electromagnetic attraction), it began to rearrange itself and start its energetic awakening. Perhaps the best way to explain this is a geometric law that states, "The sum of the parts equal the whole." Time is a human invention, and in the spiritual plane of nothingness, time did not and does not exist. We can only surmise, using our time terminology, that it took eons and eons for this awakening to occur. Eventually, this matter contemplated itself and became pure inner intelligence.

This inner intelligence or nuclei is what we call on the human plane, God, the True Source, I Am that I Am, Jehovah, Divine Spirit, Mother-Father God, etc. In this book, I have chosen to use the words "God, the True Source" because the word God has been bastardized by so many despots on this planet that I feel it has become abused and is now misunderstood by some people. For example, Hitler said God was on his side. For that reason, I prefer the term, God, the True Source, because I believe God is unconditional love and would never participate in any form of killing or harming.

In this process of contemplating itself, this matter began to expand into different forms and, through this divine process, created what scientists call the theory of the Big Bang. Scientists consider this process to be the beginning of the universe. In essence, this matter created different energy planes of existence that operated on complex frequencies and vibrations. This situation was necessary for the matter to coalesce itself into different forms and shapes. It is and was a great experiment, and eventually, it evolved into planets, black holes, suns, etc. The truth is that this grand experiment is still going on and continually evolving. Nothing in this universe is static because the universe is expanding at all times into new frequencies, vibrations, and energies. These energies and vibrations have become known as spiritual planes. God, the True Source, is ever expanding into new levels of energy, vibrations, and frequencies. These new levels are called planes of existence that contain different spiritual-energetic forms.

Our essence is an aspect of God, the True Source. We are all part of the oneness of God, the True Source, and part of our agreement when we took on human form was to share our experiences with God, the True Source. Therefore, what one of us experiences, we all experience on some level because we are all part of the same. This point is illustrated in the book *The Hundredth Monkey* by Ken Keyes, Jr.

Keyes discusses how the Japanese monkey, Macaca Fuscata, had been observed in the wild over a period of thirty years. In 1952, on the island of Koshima, scientists were providing monkeys with sweet potatoes when some of them dropped in the sand. The monkeys did not like the taste of raw sweet potatoes because they found the dirt unpleasant. An eighteen-month-old female named Imo found she could solve this problem by washing the potatoes in a nearby stream. She taught this trick to her mother. Her playmates also learned this new way and they taught their mothers as well.

This cultural innovation was gradually picked up by various monkeys before the eyes of the scientists. Between 1952 and 1958, all the young monkeys learned to wash the sandy sweet potatoes to make them more palatable. All the parents who imitated the children learned from the social improvement.

Then something startling took place. In the autumn of 1958, a certain number of Koshima monkeys were washing sweet potatoes—the exact number is not known. Let us suppose that when the sun rose one morning, ninety-nine monkeys on the Koshima Island had learned to wash their sweet potatoes. It was observed that later that morning, the hundredth monkey learned to wash potatoes. Then it happened! By that evening, every monkey in the tribe was washing sweet potatoes before eating them. The added energy of this hundredth monkey somehow created an ideological breakthrough!

The most surprising thing observed by the scientists, however, was that the habit of washing sweet potatoes then jumped over the sea…. Colonies of monkeys on other islands and the mainland began washing their sweet potatoes. What did this mean? That when a certain critical number of entities reach a new awareness, that new awareness may be communicated from mind to mind.

Although the exact number may vary, this hundredth monkey phenomenon means that only when a limited number of people know about a new way, will it remain in the conscious property of those people. But there is a point at which if only one person tunes into a new awareness, the field is strengthened so that the awareness is picked up by almost everyone. This also explains why the younger generation adapts to technology so rapidly and easily.

There is a wonderful expression I have heard frequently: "God don't make junk." I do not know where that saying came from, but I have heard it frequently. Therefore, everything, everyone, and all of us are *divine* and hold the unlimited energy of God, the True Source. In essence, we came out of a huge experiment by the Divine to experience everything that we helped create on the human plane, on the spiritual plane, and in our physical forms. In order for this to be accomplished, we had to go from pure energy and pure inner intelligence into a third dimensional physical form. Part of our agreement to come into this physical form was to fine-tune everything we have created. This process of fine-tuning is continuing and will go on for eternity. As time passed, many waves of energies, also called entities, left the bosom of what we now call God, the True Source, and by lowering their vibrations, energies, and frequencies, they took on physical forms.

Perhaps you are wondering why we had to lower our frequencies, vibrations, and energy levels to take on physical form. I guess the best way to explain it is to imagine an ice cube. If you place the ice cube in a pan under heat (energy), the ice cube will begin to melt, then boil, and then turn into steam. Eventually, the steam will rise and become invisible to the naked eye. Yet if you hold your hand up high enough above the pan, you will feel water droplets on your hand. If you were to reverse this process and imagine yourself as being the steam, which is almost or is invisible to the naked eye, and remove the heat, it would turn into droplets of water, eventually filling the pan with water. If that water were then placed in a different kind of energy and frequency, called the freezer, it would turn into a solid piece of ice. This is but an example of form and energy converting themselves from solid to steam and vice versa. I hope this explains to you how form goes from one vibration and energy into another vibration and energy and form.

Because we are all an aspect of the true source, we are all interconnected. Knowing this, in our embodiment, we are telepathically sharing our experiences with all and with God, the True Source. In this way, we are sharing our oneness with all that is and ever will be. A universal band of knowledge exists, as well as various spiritual planes where one can learn all that has ever occurred from the very beginning up to this present moment. The only limitations are the limitations we create with our own thoughts because we are feeling unworthy. That unworthiness feeling is the grand illusion, for since we are all interconnected and all part of God, the True Source, there is nothing we cannot achieve. It is well for us to remember this, for there is an old saying, "Argue for your limitations and you own them."

I suspect you are reading this book because you want to learn to achieve more—whether it is happiness or more tangible things. But before you can achieve the experiences I have explained in this book, it is important that you prepare yourself to have them. Therefore, I want to introduce you to two of the most powerful words in the universe: Dream Heaven. These words have high frequency and energy. They can raise your vibration and create a connection between you and God, the True Source. These words also serve a secondary purpose: They can help stop thought distractions—i.e., thinking about things you think you need to get done when you are trying to enter a state of relaxation and clarity.

Yes, these words are great for meditating. However, as I teach my students, when meditating upon them, it's best not to have any preconceived expectations because then you will almost certainly fall short of them. Therefore, in the exercise below, have no expectations but just continue the exercise until you complete it.

First, before you meditate, prepare yourself by collecting three simple items:

1. Two empty bowls or containers. Preferably they are made of glass, plastic, or some other non-metallic material.

2. 108 pennies, beads, dried beans, or any other kind of item, so long as it adds up to the number 108. Why 108? For several reasons: 1) It raises your conscious to get into the vibration and energy of this exercise, and 2) The number 108 is necessary to inculcate the cellular and energetic vibration out of the mundane into a higher vibration to connect

with your soul and God, the True Source. Coincidentally, in numerology, the numbers 108 adds up to a nine, which is completion.

3.   It also serves to work automatically with your soul to help you heal your mental, emotional, physical bodies. It addresses automatically the most important issues in your life in the correct order to be healed. To use a metaphor, it is like peeling an onion layer after layer after layer. This enables you to become closer at all levels, to God, the True Source.

Now that you have the 108 items, you can begin the next step. In one of the empty bowls, place all 108 of the items. Place the empty bowl near it. Now close your eyes and prepare yourself for this wonderful mantra, "Dream Heaven," which you will repeat 108 times to assist you in your meditation. This mantra has far-reaching positive effects; not only does it raise your vibration, but it contains the second most powerful words in the universe, so it helps you to achieve your intention on whatever you're trying to accomplish. In this case, each exercise that I have laid out for you in my book will assist you in achieving the desired goal. By following this mantra and the instructions with no specific intention except to raise your vibration, you will automatically be brought closer to God, the True Source. This closeness will enable you to have God, the True Source, provide you with inner guidance as well as increase your intuition, knowingness, and multi-dimensional healing.

For the exercise you are about to do, follow these steps:

1.   Focus your thoughts on what is called your third eye, the spiritual all-seeing eye. It is based above the bridge of your nose between your eyebrows at the lower part of your forehead.

2. Now ask God, the True Source, to surround you with the perfect bubble of protection in and around and about you at all times.

3. Set your intention for what you desire to achieve with this exercise, which is to become nothing.

4. Now breathe in the thought "Dream" and exhale the thought "Heaven."

5. Each time you have completed inhaling "Dream" and exhaling "Heaven," place one of the items from the full bowl into the empty bowl.

6. Continue the breathing exercises. Notice your physical body sensations and your emotions. Notice what is occurring in your third eye, physical body, and emotional body.

7. Continue until the full bowl containing the items you're counting is empty. Then you will automatically know you have completed the exercise of repeating the mantra "Dream Heaven" 108 times.

EXERCISE

Now that you've completed the Dream Heaven meditation, write down what you observed.

List eight observations you had while breathing in relation to the items below.

Third Eye

_____

_____

Physical Body Sensations

_____

_____

Emotional Body Feelings

_____

_____

What Have You Become?

_____

_____

It is important for you to continue this meditation in order to become nothing. Then you will experience something so incredible that it is difficult for me to explain and can only be felt and embraced. Repeat this exercise until you achieve becoming nothing. Then all of a sudden, you will realize you are part of everything. It's an amazing feeling and revelation. Once you become more proficient in this exercise, you will begin to see magnificent things beginning to happen in your life that, until now, you have only dreamt about.

SUMMARY

This prelude has been all about you awakening and realizing you are more than just a number or ordinary human being; you are a loving aspect of God, the True Source, whose possibilities are now. In the section that follows, we'll discover the Twelve Spiritual Laws and how they apply to your life.

PART I

THE TWELVE
SPIRITUAL LAWS

Introduction To The Twelve Spiritual Laws

"To forgive is to set a prisoner free and discover that the prisoner was you."

— Lewis B. Snedes

To understand how the universe operates and how you are yourself a part of all that is, it is necessary for you to understand the Twelve Spiritual Laws that guide the operation of the universe. In this first part of the book, we will look at each of these individual laws, how they operate, why they are in place, and how they affect you.

When you have finished, you will have achieved a full view of how the universe operates and your place within it.

CHAPTER 1

THE LAW OF LOVE

"It is love alone that leads to right action. What brings order in the world is to love and let love do what it will."

— Jiddu Krishnamuri

Love! What a complex, beautiful, and magnificent word. The energy, the glue that everything in this universe is comprised of is of one frequency, one energy, one vibration, and that is what we on this planet call Love. The poets, authors, songwriters—so many human beings—have tried to describe love, yet it is almost impossible to do so. For love is a feeling; it's an emotion; it is as an energy, a vibration, and a frequency. It's joyous; it is the exuberance of happiness and all the other adjectives you could ever think to use to describe it.

In the very beginning of creation, when in the space of nothingness, all the atoms, molecules, nuclei, protons, and particles were floating around and began to contemplate themselves, they began to be attracted to each other, and that began the process of creation through experimentation, and most importantly, that process was one of love, joy, excitement, and great anticipation. This excitement was filled with love, exposing itself to new kinds of experiences, and it began the Big Bang process. In this process, it is important to know that we, as individuals, are all an aspect of God, the True Source. That is why in the Bible it states that we were made in the image of God, the True Source. After this unification, we began our grand journey, the purpose of which was to create and re-create all kinds of various experiences, and then mentally, energetically, and telepathically, to relate our experiences to God, the True Source. This wonderful experience is still occurring.

As I said earlier, love is not easy to describe because we do not have adequate language to explain it fully. Therefore, I have thought deeply upon how to describe it for you here. The love from God, the True Source, is unyielding, unbending, undying, unconditional, and nonjudgmental. Just think of a mother and father's excitement upon seeing their child born. If you're a parent, can you remember the excitement, the joy, the proud feeling you experienced when you realized that your newborn child, that beautiful soul lying in your arms, was part of you via your DNA, cellular structure, vibrations, and energy. Your child is a perfect aspect of you just like each one of us is a perfect aspect of God, the True Source. This great and wonderful love can also be compared to how your favorite pet loves you unconditionally even when you are grouchy or mean, or when you yell or scream at it; it still unconditionally loves you. This is what the Source feels for you—unconditional love, allowingness, and nonjudgmentalness.

As humans, we will sometimes distance ourselves from God, the True Source, when we have feelings of insecurity, uncertainty, disappointment, victimization, anger, or frustration. These feelings and energies tend to bring about despair and a feeling of disconnection. Yet in my conversation with God, the True Source, I am told that *the* love is unwavering, unbending, and unyielding, and it is always there for us. Even if we cut off our conscious and or unconscious connection to God, the True Source, through the myriad of feelings we have that are not of unconditional love, we are always welcome back into the bosom of God, the True Source, and unconditionally forgiven. All we need to do is ask for forgiveness and it is given. Bear in mind, this unconditional love does not give us license to take negative action and to feel we can take advantage of this love and always receive forgiveness. In truth, we are always forgiven, but by the grand design of God, the True Source, no matter what we do, we always create karma and karmic debt. We actually asked for this karma before we became human as a way to keep track of our many lives; that way, we could take responsibility for our actions while remembering the Rule of Right Action and Correct Exchange. The Rule of Right Action and Correct Exchange merely states that everything we do is positive and for the good of all. One cannot manifest or ask for something negative, whether it concerns the situation, person, place, or condition. Correct Exchange means "paying it forward" and also assisting the True Source for some special mission when requested .Needless to say, when a crisis occurs of major importance, each one of us will know intuitively what we are to do. I will cover karma in more depth later when I discuss Spiritual Law IV: The Law of Karma. For now, just understand that there are two types of karma and karmic debt. One is best described as positive and the other is best described as challenging and bringing about growth. Either way, ultimately, both are positive and help us along our spiritual path.

Everything and everyone that exists outside the bosom of God, the True Source, is trying to re-create and feel God, the True Source's love. That is why some souls keep buying things to make them feel joyous and happy—because they are trying to replace that love so they can feel it again. In essence, they have either intentionally or unintentionally disconnected themselves from the feeling and energy of unconditional love from God, the True Source. Yet to reconnect is so simple. All we need to do is open ourselves up to receive this energy without any strings attached to it and without any preconceived expectations; then we can again be part of God, the True Source's Love.

This powerful love has another aspect which is our very essence. If you will allow it, you will heal yourself physically, mentally, and emotionally. It is the lack of love or partial lack of love in one's life that begins to affect one's health at every conceivable level of beingness.

"What you love, you empower. And what you fear, you empower. And what you empower, you attract."

— Anonymous

I would like to share a true story that happened to me several years ago that demonstrates God, the True Source's love. As was my custom, whenever I began to teach a new spiritual class, I would start to market it and its concept. I would always have anywhere from twenty to thirty or more students interested in my classes. However, the first night of this new class, as I waited with great anticipation and joy, only three souls showed up. Regardless, I did my customary introduction and answered any questions. After the class was over, I drove home. At that time, I lived approximately forty miles away from the metaphysical shop where I was introducing my new class. About two-thirds of the way home, I began to feel frustration over the class's low attendance. I pulled over to a safe spot on a two-lane road. Realizing my ego was bruised and I was disappointed, and wishing to understand what had happened, I decided to meditate and ask God, the True Source, why so few had attended. I will now share what was related to me.

God, the True Source, told me that someone was going to be coming to the class to try to destroy it and destroy me as well. This person was full of negativity and had a host of negative energy. God, the True Source, also told me that because I was doing the work of God, the True Source, I was under a perfect shield of protection. God, the True Source, said that this shield was my "armor" against what that negativity was trying to achieve. Furthermore, God, the True Source said that not only because I was doing the work of God, the True Source, but also because I am an aspect of God, the True Source, anyone who offends me offends God, the True Source. It was then I realized what great unconditional love and protection we all have from God, the True Source.

I later thought about how wonderful and joyous it is that we are unconditionally loved and protected. What a feeling of elation, security, and knowingness I experienced. I desire all of you reading this book to know that you are never alone and always loved.

I would like to share another aspect of the Law of Love. I once did an exercise in my class demonstrating the power of love. I had my students close their eyes, and I told them to imagine the thought of love and to embrace it until their whole body began to reverberate with the energy of love. Then I asked each of them to partner up with another student and project that energy to each other so that they could understand and feel the power of the vibrational frequency of love. Then I had each one of their partners volunteer to imagine being angry while the partner projected the energy of love. It was very interesting because the angry students could not maintain that energy of negativity and began to stutter and then totally surrender. Later on, the students came back to me, telling me that at work when someone was angry, they would project the love energy, and then the person who was angry would stop in the middle of a sentence and turn away. Just imagine for a moment what this world would be like if everybody were projecting that energy of love. If you embrace the energy of love, you embrace everything that is of God, the True Source, and then your life will be filled with love, joy, happiness, healing, prosperity, and much more.

If you embrace the law of love and truly understand that the law is all-encompassing and all providing—meaning that it brings perfect health, joy, happiness, prosperity, abundance, a made-in-heaven perfect mate, supportive and loving relationships, and all that your heart could ever desire and more—then all that will be eternally provided. It is the lack of unconditional love in your heart and beingness that blocks any and all of the above. I remind you that you are an aspect of the Divine, and God, the True Source, desires all things that will bring joy and happiness into your life. Since you are an aspect of the Divine—and God, the True Source, wants nothing less for itself, meaning you are a divine part of God, the True Source—you deserve nothing but the best in the broadest of terms, and you can receive that by just asking for it.

This law of love is immutable, part of your beingness, and always available for you to embrace if you will but let go, have no expectations, and know all will be provided abundantly for you. This concept was part of our birthright in our embodiment, and it has always existed from the very beginning when God, the True Source, began until this very moment, and it will continue to exist for all eternity. It is we humans who doubt this fact and, therefore, inadvertently block it. This blocking is part of the Law of Manifestation, which I will soon discuss. Even if we have incarnated into a Third World country or into poverty due to some karmic life lesson or mission or goal, that condition is temporal because as we embrace the energy of love, everything will change from lemons to honey.

If you currently feel that your life is blocked or hopeless, all you need to do is take a moment to ask to embrace the Divine's unconditional love. At the end of this chapter, there is an exercise to help you achieve this. I encourage you, whether your life is full of challenges or you feel filled with bliss, to partake in this exercise. We cannot have enough love and joy in our lives for we need to realize it is our choice to experience them. I hope you make that choice to receive God, the True Source's unconditional love. Remember, you are never judged as to whether you are worthy of this love for it is of your essence and your birthright. I encourage you to make that choice now!

I believe all us on this planet are going through a huge change. This change is all about the great awakening to realize who you are, what you are, and what your purpose for being here is all about. We are the harbingers of those souls yet to come, and by allowing God, the True Source's love to be felt and to share it with others, we will be awakening this planet and all its inhabitants. That awakening will transform a world filled with chaos, wars, diseases, illnesses, greed, and violence into the biblical Garden of Eden. Each one of us can now become the hundredth monkey. It is up to you and me and everyone else who reads this book to make this change.

FREE WILL AND FREE CHOICE

We all have free will and free choice. That choice boils down to whether or not you will embrace unconditional love, and thereby, trust, know, and believe that it will change your life forever. To choose unconditional love does not mean you are to be vulnerable, weak, or subservient. It means that you are ready to embrace your pure essence, which is also the essence of God, the True Source, and that is unconditional love. Nothing negative, including illness, anxiety, frustration, poverty, insecurity, or anything similar can exist in your life, much less consume you, as long as you are embracing unconditional love. By taking ownership of God, the True Source's unconditional love, you fill your cellular structure with the light and energy of God, the True Source, which is all-pervasive, consuming, healing, enlightening, and empowering. Now is your time to embrace it and watch the magic happen in your life, for in doing so, you embrace that of which you are a part of God, the True Source!

"They who are filled with love are filled with God itself."

— St. Augustine

EXERCISE

Ask yourself what is your definition of love and write it down.

_____

_____

_____

_____

_____

Now, before you complete the rest of the exercise, prepare yourself by practicing the Dream Heaven mantra 108 times.

After you have done the mantra, ask yourself to redefine your definition of love. Then write down the responses you have received and discovered to each one of the following statements.

_____

_____

_____

_____

_____

Ask to feel God, the True Source's divine love at the deepest cellular structure.

_____

_____

_____

_____

_____

Ask to sense and feel that divine love in the love of others all around you.

_____

_____

_____

_____

_____

Ask that divine love to fill *your multi-dimensional bodies from within and without at all levels.*

_____

_____

_____

_____

_____

SUMMARY

If you learn nothing else from this chapter, remember that you are created of love, by love, and from love, so your essence is that of love. God, the True Source's pure essence is love, and you are an aspect of the Divine, God, the True Source. All you have to do is open your heart and ask for divine unconditional love to fill your very being, including your cellular structure, your emotions, your mental body, your physical body, and everything around you. You will feel the glow of this love, and as you feel it, you will become a magnet that can attract, manifest, and bring everything into your life that brings love. This energy not only heals you and brings joy to you, but everything that exists in and around you will have the desire to make your heart sing. That is the law!

CHAPTER 2

THE LAW OF ONE

"I am you; you are me; we are one."

— Anonymous

Spend a moment thinking about this anonymous quote: "I am you; you are me; we are one."

If you paused to think about this quote, you most likely concluded that it means everything that exists in this universe is interrelated. That means every human who exists on this planet and everything else on this planet and throughout the universe is related, in a greater sense, to each other. Every rock, every piece of dirt, every tree, every plant, the sun, the moon, everything that exists is part of you, which, in turn, makes it all part of God, the True Source.

Since, as I pointed out previously, we are always communicating with God, the True Source, and our essence and very beingness is an aspect of God, the True Source, that means that no matter what color we are, what our gender is, whatever our backgrounds are, our true nature and energy comes from the same origin, God, the True Source.

This understanding begs several questions:

What is it about the human race that makes many of us not recognize our connection to God, the True Source?

Perhaps the answer is that we are not taught to understand our true essence. Our essence is that of the Divine, but we are not taught or even shown that everything in the universe, including ourselves, is part of the Divine. What if our belief system included an understanding that we are all part of the one and divinely connected in our essence to God, the True Source? If we were to understand this and apply the rules of God, the True Source—rules of right action, correct exchange, and unconditional love—this world we live in would be a different place. All positive change starts with one person at a time and begins to spread outward.

The question for each of us then is: What can I do to affect this change? List your thoughts below.

_____

_____

_____

_____

_____

Why are there different races and biological differences in the races on this planet?

To understand the question of race fully, we first need to understand that every being that exists in the universe is related to all the others; it is almost as if we are all brothers and sisters, cousins, aunts, and uncles. The fact remains that many of us, eons ago, were star-seeded and that is why we have so many different races on this planet.

You are perhaps wondering what star-seeded means. It's a term to describe how, eons ago, the original inhabitants of this planet were visited by other beings from other star systems and universes. Those original inhabitants cohabitated with the visitors, which explains the various DNAs, races, and cultures. I believe it is best for me to interject at this time a better understanding of all the different races that exist on mother Earth. In the beginning, this planet was designed by God, the True Source, as a place of healing, enlightenment, and joy. It was decided that different alien races would come to this planet and align themselves with a similar type of topography to what existed on their home planets. If their home planet was filled with cold mountains, that is where they would settle on earth. If their planet was tropical, on earth they settled in the tropical regions. They were separated by vibrations because those aliens who arrived here were evolving at different levels and energies.

Each species began the process of setting up its utopia and healing. There were times when they were able to see one another and other times when their vibrations were so different they were invisible to one another. This planet was designated as the Garden of Eden. In truth, various aliens came here to heal and reclaim their individual vibrations, frequencies, and DNA. You're perhaps wondering why that was so. It is because they had scientifically changed or eliminated those things they felt were undesirable in their race. In the process, they realized they had made a mistake. I guess an example of this can be found in *Star Trek*. Remember how Dr. Spock was a Vulcan and his species had eliminated emotions to become only analytical and logical? What is a key component and energy about the humans on this planet is that we are a planet of emotion, which makes us a very desirable species.

There are other groups of aliens who came at the same time and even later who began to experiment with other cultures' DNA and created other entities, which became undesirable. While this may seem far-fetched, there is now talk that in the very near future, families will be able to obtain the DNA for their future children that would have certain aspects they desire. For example, you desire your children to have blue eyes, be six feet tall, have high IQs, etc. It was the Martians who settled on the East Coast known as Atlantis who experimented with various DNAs to create entities that were half-human and half-animal. Some of these negative entities reincarnated in Nazi Germany and other parts of the world together to do experiments again. As time went by, various species cohabitated together, and thus, it is now that our DNA is called royalty. You are perhaps wondering what the term royalty means. It is an acronym for all the DNA we have acquired from aliens cohabitating with us over many millenniums. That is a euphemism because we have so many different alien DNAs in our embodiment that it makes us unique.

Our scientists choose to ignore this and instead look for scientific facts to justify the different types of races, based on the races' geological locations on the earth. While most of our cellular structure and DNA are similar, they are still slightly different. The fact is that this difference is because the entities that originally inhabited this earth were star-seeded, but they kept some of their original cellular structures. Even though there are differences, it is well to remember that each entity has the same essence as God, the True Source. New research shows that ancient humans had sex with non-human species.

According to a study conducted by Omer Gokcumen, an assistant professor of biological sciences at the University of Buffalo, ancient humans had intercourse with "ghost species" of "Proto Humans." Gokcumen explains that humans are only one member of a broader species named "hominis." Gokcumen found "wildly different" genes and DNA of humans living in Sub-Saharan Africa. He believes these genes can be traced back to about 150,000 years ago when ancient humans were breeding with this mysterious "ghost species." This other species is referred to by the scientific community as a "ghost species" because there are no known fossils from this species to be analyzed.

"It seems that interbreeding between different early hominid species is not the exception—it is the norm," Gokcumen was quoted as saying in the British newspaper *The Sun*. "Based on our analysis, the most plausible explanation for this extreme variation is archaic introgression—the introduction of genetic material from a 'ghost' species of ancient hominids."

Could this not be further evidence of humanoid interactions with aliens? Most likely, the *professor, not wishing to me made a fool of, used the standard term of unidentified DNA* as a "ghost species."

Why is this planet full of conflagrations (war/conflict)?

The answer to this question is simple. Many people in various countries do not fully understand the connection to the Divine and, therefore, do not appreciate the gift of life or the gift of cohesiveness and the true essence of love. Instead, they believe they are superior and wish to enforce their way of life and opinions upon all others, not realizing our true interconnection.

If there is only one God, the True Source, why are there so many different beliefs?

The followers of each belief system believe there is only one way to reconnect with God, the True Source, so it has to be their way. Their intent, for the most part, is pure; however, they have forgotten they are already part of God, the True Source, so they only need to ask to feel and see that connection. Then they will realize that they can now live their lives as they were meant to be with right action, correct exchange, and unconditional love, which will reap the harvest of all things that will bring joy to their hearts and souls.

Once again I remind you of what I mean by correct exchange. It merely means that we are to assist God, the True Source, by expressing unconditional love and compassion and assisting others to realize the connection to the Divine as well as to bring about positive loving changes.

This expression, of unconditional love and compassion, is not difficult; most of us do it every day. However, at times, specific challenges come into our lives that cause us unintentionally to deviate from that belief system. Some people see following the principles of unconditional love, compassion, and right action as a sign of weakness, so they try to take advantage of those who practice it. What these poor, weak, controlling souls who take advantage of others do not understand is that they are creating a karmic lesson either in their present lifetimes or in future lifetimes to help them fully comprehend their actions.

Those who recognize our oneness relationship to the Divine are the truly enlightened beings. These people practice the Rule of Right Action and Correct Exchange. As we become more and more aware of what constitutes right action and practice it, we find changes in our lives that are full of joy, happiness, prosperity, perfect health, and even far greater benefits. Sometimes what appears so difficult becomes so simple when we follow the basic Rule of Right Action and Correct Exchange.

It is important to remember that anything you become one with you makes you the same as it. You are its life, its breath, its soul, its energy, its love, and its total molecular structure. I believe the best way to illustrate this point is to share a couple of my experiences.

Before I started teaching classes in spirituality, I was employed as a professor at City University in Bellevue, Washington. I taught classes in business communications, economics, and marketing. One day, when I was teaching business communications at one of the school's satellite buildings, it was 90°. I knew the satellite campus had no air-conditioning, but it was required that all professors wear a suit or sport jacket, a tie, and a dress shirt. While driving in heavy traffic, I asked God, the True Source, how I would endure the heat in the building while I was teaching. I was told, "Become one with the heat. If you are the heat or one with anything, you do not feel the effects of it, but rather, you are in the flow and energy of it with comfort, joy, and happiness." I was then told to pull over to the side of the road and begin to meditate and ask to be in oneness with the heat. After I did this, I proceeded to the classroom, and much to my delight, I did not even perspire. The students could not understand how, teaching in my sport jacket, dress shirt, and tie, I could not feel the heat or perspire. My simple explanation to them was, "The heat does not bother me," which, in effect, was the truth.

In another instance, I was living in Carbonado, Washington, with my wife on a forty-acre farm. Our farm was rather remote and had only basic facilities—electric power, a septic system, and the purest water you could ever drink that came from an old abandoned coal mine. The water was loaded with calcium, so needless to say, my teeth were perfect as well as my bones. The coal mine consisted of two dams containing approximately 25,000 gallons of pure water. The first dam was composed of sacks of sand and the second of concrete.

Eventually, the water between the sacks of sand and the concrete dam became polluted so I had to clear out the sandbags and drain that area. That particular day it was 50° outside, and the temperature of the coal mine was always around 40-42°. I put on a light T-shirt and some swimming trunks and went into the water. It was cold! Then I heard that same little voice, this time telling me to become one with the water. It took me a few minutes, but I was able to achieve the process. My wife had feared my legs would turn blue and I would get sick; however, I was in the water for approximately three hours, but I did not turn blue nor get sick. I was totally comfortable. Just another example of oneness.

Let me give you one final example. Because we lived in such a remote area, we were approximately 1,600 feet above sea level and prone to sudden snow squalls. I lived about forty-five miles from my office and had to travel the last fifteen miles on a desolate two-lane road where there were no homes save mine and those of a few neighbors. That evening, it began to snow and snow and snow. By the time I got to that desolate road, two-and-a-half feet of snow were on the ground. My car was barely able to stay on the road, and tree branches were actually beginning to crack and fall from the weight of the snow. The first thing I did was ask to be protected so no harm would come to me, which was achieved. I noticed trees falling behind me and in front of me. Finally, I could go no farther. I left my car, and for the last three miles, I literally had to trudge through two-and-a-half feet of snow to reach home. I only had a medium-weight sweater on and no boots. Once again, I asked to become one with the snow and the weather. Seventy-five minutes later, I made it to the house with no ill effects, no frostbite, and feeling completely comfortable. I never even caught a cold.

I share this with you because I desire you to know that once you are in alignment with the Divine, all things are possible and can be achieved. I now teach this process in my classes so my students can achieve this oneness at any given time.

Earlier in this book, I asked each one of you to practice becoming nothing. If you faithfully did that, then by now you realize you are part of everything and everything is part of you, which reinforces the understanding and the concept of the Law of One. You are divine, so the only limitations you place upon yourself are those you have created.

"In a moment we are now forever, in one moment."

— Paul Goldman

EXERCISE

Gather up your 108 pennies, beans, or whatever item you're using and your two bowls. Now is the time to begin the process of inhaling the thought "dream" and exhaling the thought "heaven" 108 times by using the items in the first full bowl and placing each item in the empty bowl until the first bowl is empty. Then you will know that you have done this process 108 times. As you do this process, ask for three things:

1. To feel your oneness with God, the True Source.

2. To feel your oneness with the whole human race.

3. To feel your oneness with everything.

Once you have finished the process, write down any feelings or thoughts you had while you were asking.

How did you feel when you asked for oneness with God, the True Source?

_____

_____

_____

_____

How did you feel when you asked to feel your oneness with the whole human race?

_____

_____

_____

_____

How did you feel when you asked to feel your oneness with everything?

_____

_____

_____

_____

If you will faithfully follow through with this exercise, you will feel your oneness with everything, most specifically the Divine.

Once you have completed this oneness process, you will find that all things are possible and that the only limitations you will have in your life are those of self-imposed limitations. Of course, the Rule of Right Action and Correct Exchange applies to everything you do.

Finally, I would like you to consider this last thought. So many things are going on in our world right now that focus on issues of diversity and different cultures, and so many opinions are causing a great deal of emotional problems. Consider this: If we removed the skin on our bodies, all we would have would be our bones. Could we then tell one race from another? Perhaps you could tell whether you are male or female, but not what race or color you are or where they came from. What are your opinions on race now?

SUMMARY

It is important for all of us to remember that we are all aspects of God, the True Source. Our essence is still the oneness with the Divine, no matter who, what, or where we are, or what our culture is. Our true essence is no different from anyone else's; except for our exteriors, we are all the same. Once you realize you are part of everything that has ever existed, does exist, and will exist, then you will realize there are no limitations in your life except for those you have placed upon yourself. Your oneness with love, joy, perfect health, healing, prosperity, abundance, family, relationships, and all that you do will come into perfect alignment. That alignment will allow you to achieve your greatness, mission, and goal on the human and spiritual planes.

I encourage you to reflect upon this and feel your connection to others and to all that exists.

"Consider your own place in the universal oneness of which we are all a part, from which we all arise, and to which we all return."

— David Fontana

CHAPTER 3

THE LAW OF MANIFESTATION
A.K.A.
THE LAW OF ATTRACTION

"We are what we think....
All that we are,
Arises with our thoughts.
With our thoughts we make our world."

— **Buddha**

Perhaps the best way to explain the Law of Manifestation is with a quote from Gary Zukav: "Every intention sets energy into motion, whether you are conscious of it or not."

It is important to understand that all manifestation is the result of the Law of Electromagnetic Attraction. In essence, as you think, so you create. Every word and every thought you have expressed or thought of silently or otherwise is eventually created in your life. Think for a minute how many thoughts you have over an hour's time. I would suspect they are in the hundreds or more, and each one of those thoughts will eventually arise into your life. The reason I am pointing this out to you is that thoughts manifest into things.

One of the magnificent gifts we help to create with God, the True Source, is the freedom to manifest in our lives whatever we so desire to experience. The Law of Attraction/Manifestation does not differentiate between the positive and negative. Rather, it just fulfills each individual's manifestation. Look at it this way: Let's say you had an electrical wire that you used to power your toaster. If you tore away the insulation on the electrical wire and the toaster was plugged in, and then you proceeded to touch the wire, you could electrocute yourself, thus causing your demise. Electricity in its purest form is neutral; however, how you use it can be positive or negative. The same is true with thought. Your thoughts/manifestations can be one or the other, positive or negative.

The secret to a successful manifestation consists of two parts: 1) the strength of your intent, focus, imagination/and or ability to visualize, concentration, and 2) your understanding that you are entitled to whatever you create. The only thing that will enhance or block your manifestation is how deserving you feel of that particular manifestation. Everything in this universe is here for us to experience. No limitations exist on manifesting anything you so desire to experience, so long as your desire is stated with right action and correct exchange. Right action demands you never manifest out retribution or, to use a phrase, "want a pound of flesh."

I cannot tell you how many souls I have encountered over the years who have had problems manifesting what they desire because of their lack of belief that they are deserving or that they can achieve it. A lot of this lack of belief comes from the programming in our lives either from our families, peers, or from even our feelings of unworthiness.

As an example, I would like to tell you the story of two of my students. They were a beautiful couple in their fifties who were struggling financially. I had explained to them numerous times how to manifest a better life of prosperity and joy than what they were currently experiencing. They were not successful, and I could not understand why. Finally, out of frustration, I asked them what they felt was occurring in their lives that was blocking their manifestation. The husband told me that his great-great-grandfather had married outside his religion, and as a result, his father cursed him saying that he would never be financially successful; so he struggled financially for the rest of his life. His belief accentuated that curse, and he passed that belief onto his son, who passed it onto his son, and then finally onto his son, my client.

I had a long talk then with this couple to explain to them that everything that exists is ours to experience as long as it is right action and correct exchange. Nothing can stop the manifestation of right action and correct exchange except our own doubts and a belief in our unworthiness. He replied that he could understand this concept, but then he referred to the history of his father, grandfather, and great-grandfather, etc. I explained to him that their belief system had been passed on and was not created by God, the True Source; I then asked him, "If they had believed that God, the True Source, was unconditionally loving, allowing, and nonjudgmental, why would prosperity and abundance have been prevented from coming into their lives?" Obviously, he had no answer.

Next, I explained to this couple that 94 percent of our thinking comes from the subconscious mind and only 6 percent from the conscious mind. Therefore, when the conscious mind thinks or believes something positive, it appears to the person as if it is a done deal, so to speak; however, whatever is embedded in the subconscious/ unconscious mind always takes precedence. In the subconscious/

unconscious mind, things are either positive or negative; there is no gray area, while in the conscious mind, there is positive, neutral, and negative. I then asked them whether there was any reason they could come up with for why they had created a powerful negative karma in this lifetime that would prevent them from achieving the prosperity and abundance they so desired. They could come up with nothing. My next step was for them to write down all the reasons they were undeserving of prosperity and abundance, and then, on a separate sheet of paper, write down all the reasons they were worthy of prosperity and abundance. They could only come up with a few reasons why they were unworthy, but they struggled to find reasons why they were worthy. As I discussed the reasons why they were worthy and asked them to block out any thoughts of unworthiness, the positive list became longer and longer.

I teach several powerful affirmations to help manifest various individual desires. The first I taught them was, "I am not my body. I am not my past. I am!" The next I suggested they use was "I am unlimited!" I instructed them to say this manifestation thirty-six times a day in front of the mirror, including just before going to sleep. Perhaps you are wondering, *Why the mirror?* It's because everything you say in front of the mirror is energetically said and reflected back into your very beingness more than a hundredfold. Think about these aforementioned statements and you will realize that you are the sole (soul) creator of your life, that your thoughts are powerful, and that you are unlimited in creating anything you so desire to experience in your life, with no differentiation of positivity or negativity in the manifestation.

God, the True Source, also gave me this wonderful manifestation that I want to pass on to you now: "The past predicts the present, and the present predicts the future." Therefore, if you live in the past with negativity, that negativity will continue to manifest itself in the present and in the future; conversely, if you live in the past with positivity, it will continue to manifest in the present and the future. It is a very simple formula that can be changed at any time. It matters not whatever negativity occurred in the past; if you change the present to positivity, then positivity will also manifest in the future. Technically speaking, the future is less than a nanosecond away. You become the change you want to be.

So what happened to this couple who believed they were under a family curse? Their life slowly changed, and they were able to purchase a house, a new car, and to travel. Their perceived curse was over and now gone forever. They also learned a lesson that whatever their belief system was would determine what they attracted into their lives. If you follow and believe in the Law of Manifestation/Attraction, then everything is possible, including love, perfect health, prosperity, joy, and your made-in-heaven miracle mate (more about him/her a little later).

You may now be wondering, *How do I stop or prevent a negative manifestation?* The answer is simple: First, you need to pay attention to your thoughts and words. Secondly, if the negative thought or words come forth, you need to be aware of them and begin this simple process. After you realize you have expressed the negative thoughts or words, it is imperative that you utter this statement three times: Cancel. Cancel. Cancel. Understand that saying this three times is a manifestation in itself, blocking and preventing the negative thoughts and/or words. Since there is no vacuum in the universe, you must replace that thought with a positive thought; otherwise, the original thought will come back into your life at some time. It is important to remember that all manifestations will come into reality at your perfect time; this is important to realize because sometimes we desire the manifestation to arrive yesterday. It is best to remember to manifest something before lack of it becomes a crisis in your life. The reason is if you try to manifest it in a crisis, you will have two opposing thoughts: 1) that it will occur, and 2) energy or belief that it is hopeless. Remember, the subconscious mind will always overcome the conscious mind. I have explained this previously. It is highly advisable that when you are manifesting something in your life, you do it in concert with the Divine. God, the True Source, always told me that when you manifest something in your life in concert with God, the True Source, it will be achieved at God, the True Source's perfect time for you. I shall explain this in more depth in the ensuing paragraphs as I share some key stories that illustrate the power of working with God, the True Source, and manifestation.

The next story is about one of my students who was a single mom. She had two children and was always living paycheck to paycheck. In order to pay her rent, she filed her income taxes early so she could get a refund. After she sent in her income tax forms, she realized she had forgotten to add additional deductions that would have more than paid for the rent. She came to me in a panic and asked me what to do. I told her to file an addendum to her income tax and mail it immediately. We then did a manifestation asking God, the True Source, to assist in obtaining her income tax refund before her rent was due. She had only ten days in which to achieve this manifestation. I told her not to worry because it would occur in the Divine's perfect time, which would also be her perfect time. The following week when she came to class, she said she had been repeating the manifestation multiple times each day. By the morning of the third day, she clearly heard a voice say: "I heard you. I heard you. I heard you." A few days later, she called me to say she had received the income tax refund in time to pay her rent. Needless to say, she was elated, as was I, and we both gave thanks to God, the True Source.

"What you think…and what you feel…and what manifests is always a match, every single time! No exception."

— **Esther Hicks**

Another time, the home of a student of mine was about to be auctioned off for nonpayment of IRS taxes. He needed two additional weeks to raise the money, but the IRS refused to grant him this time. We did a manifestation that he would not lose his home but instead would obtain the money required to satisfy the IRS debt. I reminded him, "It will happen not in our time but in the Divine's perfect time for you, and you need to trust." The auction was in four days. The following week, he came to class very elated and told me a wonderful story. The auctioneer had become ill, so he could not perform the auction for three weeks. Obviously, my student was able to raise the money in this time and save his home. The lesson here is that we cannot determine nor anticipate how something will work out; rather, we just have to accept it is going to manifest perfectly into our life. There is always that cliché, "God, the True Source, works in mysterious ways." This story was certainly an example of it.

This last story is truly an amazing one. I am a nondenominational minister, and one day, I was performing a wedding at a very exclusive country club. My wife at the time was a cancer survivor, and her hair was just beginning to grow back. The woman in charge of the wedding asked me whether my wife was a cancer survivor. When I said yes, she told me she was also a cancer survivor, and five years ago, she had been given six months to live. I looked at her and marveled at how beautiful and complete she looked. I asked her what was her secret. She told me she had prayed and begun to imagine she was running through a meadow barefoot and totally and completely healed. She did this several times a day, and after six months, she was still alive and totally and completely healed. She had faith in the Divine that whatever was best for her would be achieved. She had no expectations, but simply lived each moment of the day the best she could. What a powerful manifestation she created.

Obviously, the lesson from all of these stories is that once we perform the manifestation, we need to get out of our own way and let God, the True Source, bring it forth, at perfect timing for us and in the best way. As a human, our basic problem is learning to trust; that has always been a challenge with many souls. Perhaps because of various experiences in our lives, certain things have not come to fruition; therefore, we have skewed our belief systems. Yet I believe that if we really examine those things that we may have tried to manifest but that did not occur, we will realize they may not have been for our best and highest good, even though, intellectually, we thought they would be. I have encountered so many beautiful souls who have been angry about their lives and feel nothing good or positive will ever occur for them. With that attitude, they block the beautiful manifestations they are entitled to experience. With every-thing we do in life, there is a payoff. If one is doing negative things or is jealous, envious, angry, hateful, or revengeful, the payoff will be whatever that person is feeling or expressing. On the other hand, if the soul is expressing love, joy, happiness, assistance, caring, compassion, charity, or any type of love, the result will be exactly that.

As humans, we are experts at creating experiences that are painful or experiences that are loving and joyful. Essentially, we are in control of the type of life we desire to experience. It is our responsibility as individuals to create the life and experiences we so desire unconditionally, for, you see, God, the True Source, is unconditionally loving, nonjudgmental, and allowing! It is clearly understood by the Divine that whatever you are manifesting in your life is something that is causing you to grow, understand, heal, and, eventually, empower yourself. In other words, we all have free will and free choice. It is incumbent upon each individual soul to choose in which direction he or she will desire to have his or her experiences.

Living a life knowing that all things are possible will help you achieve anything and everything you so desire.

"Whether you think you can or whether you think you can't, you're right."

— Henry Ford

ENERGY

To understand manifestation further, it is best to understand energy. Everything in this universe equates to energy. The universe contains many types of energy; for example: love, joy, happiness, hate, envy, poverty, prosperity, insecurity, fear, anger, anxiety, loneliness, depression, insecurity, victimization, insecurity, self-worth, health, and many more. As I have said previously, all thought is electromagnetic, meaning we individually attract into our lives our thoughts, and eventually, those thoughts become things. It is important for each of us to remember we are indeed the creators of our lives. In some instances, we bring these energies into our lives to learn karmic lessons and/or karmic debts. If we realize that everything is mutable, then we have the power to change positivity into negativity or negativity into positivity. Perhaps you are wondering how this can be done. One of the grand lessons that God, the True Source, has taught me is to look at how you created something in your life and then, by reversing it, uncreate it. A perfect example of this was the story I told you earlier about the couple who felt they had a curse and could never achieve prosperity. It took four generations to realize that they could undo that misconstrued belief that the family would never be prosperous and successful. As I said, that couple did achieve prosperity and abundance in their life. They reversed the situation by changing the affirmation from being a curse to one of believing they are deserving along with a belief system that God, the True Source desires everything for them in a unconditional loving way. It can best be explained by the term reverse engineering.

Take a moment to understand and figure out how you manifested a specific situation either intentionally or inadvertently. Once you are able to understand the mechanics of what you have created, you can manifest the opposite of it. As in the above example, they reversed the curse into a nonissue and re-manifested positivity in their life by changing their belief system to one that says they are now able to create prosperity and abundance. This simple principle can be applied to any manifestation/thought to reverse-engineer a situation in your life that is untenable or to enhance your life.

Since all energy in its essence is neutral, except for the energy of Love, how something is expressed in our lives depends solely on how we interpret, accept, or reject our thoughts. It is important not only to express a thought but to embrace it (energetically) in order to feel its full effects. All energy that comes into our lives that is expressed as a positive or negative is done in one of two ways: 1) by constant repetition, or 2) by shock. Constant repetition embeds the energy into our subconscious and cellular structure. A "shock" causes a physical response. That response could either be a physical reaction, such as an electrical jolt coming into your body, or the acceptance of some kind of blocking fear in its totality. Understanding these two methods can explain our behaviors. That is why when mantras and affirmations are consistently repeated, they produce a desired positive result because the shock value of a belief system/manifestation is more quickly integrated into the conscious/unconscious mind and physical body.

Let me give you an example of how the shock value works. I have a client who called me one day and told me she was unable to balance her checkbook. I asked her what had happened. She said she had messed up the checkbook and her husband called it to her attention. He kept telling her she was dumb at math and couldn't balance the checkbook. After making repetitive mistakes in the checkbook for several weeks, it appeared that she was unable to keep it accurately. I asked her how she felt about that. She said she felt hurt and surprised because this had not occurred before. I asked her what she did for a living. She told me she was a mortgage broker. I asked her once again whether her computations were correct when she presented the numbers and documents to the underwriters for approval. She told me yes, she was always correct. All of a sudden, as if a light bulb went off in her head, she said, "I've got it" and never had a problem balancing the checkbook again. That is an example of something coming into your field of energy through a shock.

Let me discuss in more detail how this energy works. Have you ever noticed how some people are extremely prosperous, lucky, and successful while others just plod along, living day to day, moment to moment, and are always unhappy, complaining, and acting like victims?

In the first scenario, when a person is extremely prosperous, lucky, and successful, that person believes without a doubt that anything he or she undertakes will be successful and that it will be achieved with grace and ease. There is no doubt in the person's minds that this will occur. In essence, you are embracing and projecting the energy that enables you to achieve your desired outcome. In the second scenario, where someone is living day to day, moment to moment, and is always unhappy, complaining, and acting like a victim, the energy that person is embracing and projecting is also drawing negative situations into that person's life. So what does this tell us? It tells us we have a choice to live in self-created blocks or in self-created unlimitedness. We have a choice to embrace our limits or be limitless.

That choice always exists no matter what life we have been born into or have created. If, for example, a woman is going to a party and she feels inadequate or second-class and, therefore, unworthy, she will be treated that way. However, if she will embrace the thought that she is a beautiful, positive, wonderful soul, she will attract a great deal of attention, and the desired result, no matter what her physical attributes are. The same applies to males. There is an old saying that if you hang out with successful people, you will become successful, and conversely, if you hang out with those whose perceptions are of victimization and loss, you will become that.

The problem with our human nature is that we want everything yesterday. We forget that whatever negativity exists in our life did not occur instantaneously, but rather, over a period of time. The same applies to positivity. When you have been negative and, figuratively speaking, you switch gears, it will take time for the change to manifest in your life. All things that you have created, both positive and negative, will constantly be re-created in your life as long as you embrace that thought in your life.

When desiring to manifest something, it is important to remember that we must not concentrate on how it is to be accomplished, but rather, on the end result. Imagine for a minute that you desire a specific new car. You do the work to manifest it; you embrace it, feel it, and even imagine driving it and how it feels when it accelerates. It is unimportant how the vehicle comes into your life because if you place conditions on it for how it will appear, you may block it or slow it down from coming into your life. It is more important that you achieve the desired result, which, in this case, is that vehicle.

I am friends with a married couple who, every time they move, always has to have a home with a covered patio. I don't know whether they are aware of this, but they created the first patio several years ago in their first home because they wanted to enjoy sitting out in the evening and being protected from the elements; consequently, each successive home has always had a covered patio. I know they are not consciously manifesting it, but they are doing so unconsciously. So far, they have had three homes with covered patios. I point this out so you will understand that we are consciously and unconsciously manifesting those things in our lives that bring us both challenges and joy.

It is best to remember that you never have an insurmountable block in your life; the connotation of insurmountable is something that can never be overcome, and if you feel that way, you will create your own Mount Kilimanjaro. However, if you change your thinking to seeing the situation as a challenge, then you have the connotation that it can be overcome with little or no effort. It is what we think of it—whether we view it as difficult or easy—that enables us to overcome the challenge with difficulty or ease. Once again, the choice is yours. It behooves us to be around positive souls rather than the negative naysayers or those who are so embedded in negativity that they wish to draw us down to their low levels.

You are the sum total of everything that has occurred in your life. Is it not wonderful, then, that we have choices, and that through patience, concentration, and embracing our desired outcome, we can achieve our dreams? It is also best that if you have children, you desire for them to be happy, joyous, successful, healthy, prosperous, and much, much more. Since you are an aspect of God, the True Source, nothing less than that is what the Divine desires for you. There is no difference between what you desire for your children as a parent and what God, the True Source, desires for you. It is important for you to embrace this, own this, and now become this. For, you see, the only limitations in your life are those that you have either taken ownership of, created, or allowed to control you. Is it not great to know that you are the captain of your own ship? What is even more important is that you are an example for your children, your family, your friends, your relatives, and all those around you.

At times, we may we wish to emulate others because of the beautiful things they are doing in their lives. Instead, why not be the example for them to emulate—the example that brings joy, happiness, and success into their lives. Remember, if your life is going awry, you created it, so now it's a time to uncreate it! Congratulations! You have just taken your first step toward changing your life in a positive way to achieve your dreams. One of my favorite quotes that I termed is:

"The past is but an experience.
The present is but a moment.
The future is but a thought."

Take a moment to reflect on what you have just read, realizing that you are deserving of everything that is beautiful, positive, and joyous in your life, no matter what it may be. Fully understand that you are the sole (soul) creator of it. Embrace that thought, take ownership of it, and you will quickly become it.

You have a choice to realize that you are an antenna that is broadcasting its emotions, both positive and negative. One of the things you need to do is broadcast love and joy, happiness, and all kinds of positivity. Not only do you need to broadcast those positive emotions for everything around you, but also for your mental, emotional, physical, and energetic health to increase your life force's energy. Understanding how you broadcast is very important because your energy and thoughts affect your loved ones, all of your surroundings, and everything that exists on this planet in any shape and form. Even Mother Earth has an intelligence of her own, so she will also pick up on your thoughts and emotions and they will influence her own, which can affect this entire planet both positively and negatively. Just look at the world and the problems we see—if there is drought, it is a reflection of our thoughts and emotions. I remember one time radio broadcaster Art Bell brought up the subject of an area in the United States that was sorely in need of rain. Art Bell asked his listeners to spend a few moments using their thoughts and consciousness en masse to ask for rain in that particular area. A couple of days later, such a huge deluge of rain fell in that area that it caused severe flooding. In this case, there was no guideline or judgment given as to whether there should be a little rain or a lot of rain, flooding or no flooding. The lesson for Art Bell and all of us is that we can create thoughts that attract and become reality. In retrospect, if they had manifested with grace, harmony and ease, everything would have been in balance.

Therefore, when we think of something or verbalize it or write it, it is a manifestation. Consequently, when you seek to manifest something, ask that it be achieved with grace and ease, love and joy, happiness and harmony, and balance and perfect protection for all involved. It is important for each one of us to remember to ask this when we are manifesting and creating something positive in our lives or in others' lives. By doing this, the desired outcome will be very positive. Is it not wonderful to realize that your consciousness is tied in with that of other souls and that it has the power, the gift, and the ability to create positive, wonderful, loving changes? But it is necessary that we remember when manifesting that it be done with a focus on love, joy, and happiness because others out there are sending contrary or negative thoughts for whatever reasons they may have, and those thoughts are usually all about control and manipulation of the masses. Therefore, after the manifestation of positive thoughts for the mass consciousness or individual consciousness, turn over those thoughts to God, the True Source, for *right action and correct exchange*. When you do this, you will come to the realization that everything happens in God, the True Source's perfect timing and not ours!

I would like to share a story of how I learned to manifest with love, grace, and ease. One day, I decided that my body needed a cleansing. I asked for it to be thoroughly cleansed. As a result, I frequently had to use the bathroom for three days. I then realized that I had forgotten to say I wanted it to happen with love, grace, and ease. Although it is quite humorous when I look back upon it, I did cleanse myself; I just could have made it a lot easier for myself. The way I manifested it made it very difficult to carry on an intelligent conversation with someone because of the obvious interruptions. Plus, the classes I was teaching would have been a lot easier to teach if I hadn't had to keep running to the restroom. When I explained my situation to my students, they thought it was hilarious.

You may now be wondering what are the limitations for manifesting whatever you desire in life. There are none! You have the ability, gift, and power to manifest whatever you desire. I cannot stress enough that when you seek to manifest, you must always, always, always ask for it to be done with love, joy, harmony, balance, and ease. I know I'm being repetitive here, but I want to emphasize this point because asking for the manifestation to occur in a positive manner is such an important ingredient. As I mentioned earlier, 94 percent of our thinking comes from our subconscious mind and only 6 percent comes from our conscious mind. The 94 percent in the subconscious mind controls our life, either positively or negatively. The 6 percent from the conscious mind is always being negated by the subconscious mind if they are not in harmony. As I brought up before, let us suppose you have an addiction to something; you wake up in the morning and say, "I am going to give up this addiction." The subconscious mind, which thinks in black and white, says, "No, you're not going to give up this addiction because it serves a purpose you have created." Your subconscious does not judge whether it is positive or negative; it just receives information and ask the outcome to be manifested. We need to look at our lives and realize what is controlling us that we have taken ownership of; then we will know why the subconscious mind keeps repeating the same negative block. Furthermore, the subconscious mind is more active and repeats thoughts continually. Conversely a positive subconscious mind will manifest more quickly on a continuing basis until you change it.

By comparison, the conscious mind thinks in black, white, and gray, but it also isn't as active; consequently, you have to exert yourself more by repeating things consciously. Eventually, those conscious positive thoughts you repeat will become subconscious positive thoughts. Then if you have a conscious negative thought, because the subconscious has more positive thoughts, it will negate the negative thought. Therefore, if you spend more time focusing on your conscious thoughts and making them positive, you will increase your likelihood for happiness and your ability to manifest what you truly want in your life.

Do you realize now how powerful you are? Your thoughts control your world, but you can control your thoughts. It's important, therefore, to understand that all thoughts are energy; you are energy, and everything that exists is energy. Energy has an intelligence of its own, and how you use that energy determines how it will manifest in your life. For example, electricity is a neutral energy that can be used for light, cooking, baking, heating water, and even more. If you view energy as positive, you are 100 percent correct. But what happens if you touch electrical wires? Then energy can become a destructive force. It can end lives and start fires. Therefore, you need to focus on creating positive energy in your life.

Let's return to our imagining of ourselves as huge antennae. Everything you think is being broadcasted from your body out into the ethers. Everything you feel, say, imagine, or express is sent out to the ethers. Therefore, it is important to look at your body and all the components of it as if it were a radio/TV station sending out all types of information. As an antenna, you not only send out energy but you also receive it. Have you ever experienced being in a great mood and everything is going well, when all of a sudden, everything comes to a crashing end and you become depressed, anxiety-ridden, unhappy, or insecure? That happens when you pick up energy from souls you are close to or from certain situations occurring on this planet.

Many souls are empaths who pick up energy; their primary job is to take away the physical, mental, and/or emotional pain from others and pass it on to be cleansed and healed by God, the True Source. As an empathic healer, I know it is important to remember that the energy must be transmuted from your physical being to be cleansed and healed. By just asking God, the True Source, to cleanse and clear you of this energy, it will automatically be done. Presently, so much chaos is happening in this world that as antennae, we are picking up on that energy and it is affecting our lives in very many challenging ways. And you have a choice to say, "I am creating my emotions, positive or negative. One thing I need to do is work on myself so I can enjoy the happiness I have created and share it with everybody around me." It is necessary that you do this for your own physical, mental, and emotional health, and that you realize what you think and project will affect everything—from our loved ones to all the beings on this planet. Don't forget that Lady Gaia, also known as Mother Earth, has an intelligence of her own, so she will reflect human emotions. For example, where there is drought, Mother Nature is feeling emotions of anxiety and frustration and manifesting drought in that area as a result.

BIBLICAL PROOF OF UNLIMITED PROSPERITY AND ABUNDANCE

For an example of a positive manifestation turning into negativity, let's consider a person who is manifesting prosperity into her life. Let's say the prosperity she asked for arrives and continues to flow more and more. Then, suddenly, something happens where she loses some money, either by a bad decision or something along those lines, and she becomes fearful. As a result, she begins to take ownership of that fear, and the new manifestation of fear, unintentionally, blocks further prosperity and abundance in her life. Another example would be a man who learned from his parents that money burns a hole in your pocket and is impossible to hang onto. He might even have come to believe that if he gets extra money, it means something will go wrong, such as his car breaking down, so he'll lose that money anyway. Because this man thinks, *I cannot enjoy the extra money*, guess what—he manifests that as his reality.

Understand that no matter what you manifest, if it suddenly turns negative even for a moment and you take ownership of it, it will become either that which you fear or that which you love—whichever is the greater, more positive, powerful thought. It is incumbent upon you to remember that God, the True Source, wants you to have a life of love, joy, happiness, perfect health, unlimited prosperity, and much more. The Old and New Testaments provide many examples to verify this truth. Here are a few of them:

"Beloved, I wish above all things that thou may prosper."

— 3 John 1:2

"Prove me now herewith, Said the Lord Of hosts, if I will not open you the windows Of heaven And pour you out a blessing that there shall not be room enough to receive it."

— Malachi 3:10

"The blessing of the Lord, It maketh rich, and He addeth no sorrow with it."

— Proverbs 10:22

"They shall prosper that love Thee. Peace be within thy walls, and prosperity within thy palaces."

— Psalms 122:6-7

"The LORD shall open unto thee his good treasure, the heaven to give the rain unto thy land in his season, and to bless all the work of thine hand: and thou shalt lend unto many nations, and thou shalt not borrow."

— Deuteronomy 23:12

> *"All things whatsoever ye pray and ask for, Believe that ye have received them And ye shall have them."*
>
> **— Mark 11:24**

Many of the greatest and most inspiring minds from human history have also verified the truth of these statements. Here are just a few examples:

> *"Man was born to be rich, or inevitably grows rich by the use of his faculties, by the union of thought with nature."*
>
> **— Ralph Waldo Emerson, American author and philosopher**

> *"The world, with all its beauty, its happiness and suffering, its joys and pains, is planned with the utmost ingenuity, in order that the powers of the Self may be shown forth in manifestation."*
>
> **— Annie Besant, British writer, women's rights activist, and theosophist**

> *"What we need to realize above all else is that God has provided for the most minute needs of our daily life, and that if we lack anything it is because we have not used our mind in making the right contact with the supermind and the cosmic ray that automatically flows from it."*
>
> **— Charles Fillmore, American mystic and founder of the Unity church**

Somehow or other, through time, many of these quotes have been buried or not expressed. However, we now have the opportunity to read them and realize that with love and by requesting God, the True Source, to fulfill our manifestations, all things shall be given to us.

Reflect on this thought that all things are possible. Prosperity and manifestation go hand-in-hand. Our upbringing and, in some cases, our religious teachings and background are what create limitations in our lives, not only for prosperity and abundance, but also for perfect health, love, joy, and happiness.

It is important at this point for each of us to realize that since we are aspects of God, the True Source, all things that are beautiful, wondrous, and joyous were created by God, the True Source, and are ours for the partaking. They are open for us to experience. For life on earth is nothing but an experience, and anything we have created or that has been created, whether eons ago or moments ago, can be recreated instantaneously. If you can manifest a penny, you can manifest unlimited wealth, for it takes no more or less energy to manifest a penny than it does to manifest unlimited wealth or health, joy, happiness, or anything else that brings us pleasure in your life. The energy for something small is the same as the energy for something humongous. It only involves love, joy, and happiness in the realization that you deserve anything and everything in your life. As I said previously, you're here to experience everything; hopefully, you will now desire to experience everything positive.

EXERCISE

Take time to write down a list of the greatest fears, doubts, and challenges in your life.

_____

_____

_____

_____

Prepare for your meditation by breathing Dream Heaven 108 times as before.

Now, if possible, try to ascertain how those negatives came into your life so you can begin the process of un-creating them as I have described.

_____

_____

_____

_____

Ask God, the True Source, to assist you in releasing these blocks in your life. Realize you are now uncreating/reverse-engineering them by embracing the energy of a positive outcome through positive thoughts. Now become both thoughts, embracing and feeling the energy, love, joy, happiness, and completion of those thoughts. List them now and ask for healing.

_____

_____

_____

_____

It is time to wake up from your deep slumber to realize this is the world you have created. Take a moment or two to embrace that fact; look upon the wonderful things you have created and the challenges you have created. It is important to realize everything you do, every breath, every thought, every action, every subconscious thought, every word will now come into your field of energy and manifest forth. Look how powerful and creative you are! Are you ready to make a change? Are you ready to enhance your life and improve upon those things that bring you love and joy? Are you ready to uncreate and release all that is a block or an impediment in your life? Realize that every block, every impediment, every negative thought, every illness, is created by your programming from either your family and friends' religious backgrounds, fears, doubts, insecurities, negative self-worth, negative self-love, or negativity in your life. Know that these great obstacles are no longer obstacles but challenges to overcome by quickly changing your thoughts and attitudes and realizing you are deserving! Now is the time to begin to make those changes. Now is the time to *create* the life you deserve and have dreamt of. The choice is clear: remain stuck or change not only for you but for your family and future children. It is now. So be it!

"All that we are is the result of what we have thought.
If a man speaks or acts with an evil thought, pain follows him.
If a man speaks or asks with a pure thought, happiness follows him,
like a shadow that never leaves him."

— Buddha

EXERCISE

Make a list of what you have created with your thoughts that has created challenges in your life.

_____

_____

_____

_____

_____

Make a list of joyous things that have occurred in your life up to this point.

_____

_____

_____

_____

_____

_____

_____

After examining both lists, realize that you are the sole creator and manifester of these lists. The objective is to realize you can create anything in your life you desire, and why not create those things that bring love, joy, happiness, prosperity, abundance, perfect health, and even much more!

SUMMARY

It is important that you realize you are the sole (soul) creator of your life. Employ the techniques of realizing that you are worthy and that everything in existence is yours to enjoy. You are an unlimited person who can create or recreate a life that brings fulfillment. Remember, all thoughts are things and you are in charge. Reread this chapter and apply the understanding and techniques. Bless you; know you are divine!

CHAPTER 4

THE LAW OF KARMA

"Contrary to popular misconception, karma has nothing to do with punishment and reward. It exists as part of our holographic universe's binary or dualistic operating system only to teach us responsibility for our creations—and all things we experience are our creations."

— **Sol Luckman**

Karma is nothing but an experience; it is neither good nor bad, for only our interpretation of it makes it one way or the other. In truth, karma is an experience to empower us no matter how we interpret it. If you take a moment to think about this, you will realize what an ingenious concept it is. For God, the True Source's wisdom allows each one of us to practice free will and free choice and to bear or enjoy the fruit of our choices. Therefore, it is easy to understand that the Divine does not punish us, create disharmony, create loss or illness, or create any of the other negative things we think we are being punished or even rewarded for. As a dear friend of mine would say, "What is the payoff?" In physics, we know that for every action, there is a reaction, and so that applies to our life as well.

In order for us to grow spiritually, we have chosen, individually, to experience everything so that we can understand compassion, love, joy, and happiness in our lives. How can you know what cold is until you touch an ice cube, and how can you know what hot is until you have touched a hot pot? How can you understand joy without comparing it to unhappiness, or know what love is without experiencing it? It's important to know that these experiences are empowering, and they only need to be in your life for as long as you desire them to be. If you live in the past, you become chained to the past and do not grow. If you live in the present, you experience everything around you that is able to help you grow. If you live in the future, it is only an illusion that has not come to reality yet and, therefore, can imprison you in your thoughts and prevent you from growing. Everything that has existed in your life up to this point, you have created for an experience. You may ask yourself, "Why would that soul choose the experience of being a paraplegic or having some illness or other debilitating situation?" In simple terms, these are experiences to allow people to understand compassion, joy, love, and whatever else is necessary for each person to grow.

I knew a beautiful soul who developed multiple sclerosis. She was quite perplexed why it had occurred in her life. At that time, she was receiving no love from her husband or others around her; therefore, she decided, before incarnation, to receive the lesson of love by developing multiple sclerosis, and eventually, she then allowed a wonderful loving experience into her life. In her previous lifetime, she had been treated poorly and felt unloved so this disease was what her way of carrying that karma into this lifetime. By contracting multiple sclerosis, she finally understood what it is to feel love, appreciation, and joy in her life. We might judge her illness as a hard lesson, and I guess that, looking at the surface of it, it is. But when you look at the big picture, you can see what a beautiful choice she made to understand and experience what love is all about. In her next lifetime, she most likely will not need to experience such an illness since she is currently learning the lesson.

Here are some more examples of how karma works. Some people have gathered extreme wealth into their lives, and in some instances, this wealth is the result of karma; for example, they may have given away their wealth to others in a previous life so now they are being rewarded, or they may have been poor in a past life, so now it is time for them to experience prosperity. Similarly, other people in a past life may have had low self-worth and self-esteem; they chose to learn that lesson by becoming alcoholics, being addicted to drugs, having multiple marriages, etc. Once they learn that lesson, in future lives, they may be very self-confident, so they will focus, instead, on learning another lesson.

So far, I've addressed karmic experiences we have brought into this lifetime to heal and empower ourselves. But there are other karmic experiences we create on a daily basis. Let's suppose that rather than honoring your body's needs and limitations, you overindulge with food, so you end up being overweight. The karmic reaction may be diabetes, high blood pressure, ulcers, rebuilt knees, or rebuilt hips. Perhaps you are the type of person who likes to control everything in your life, so you end up with osteoporosis or severe arthritis.

I would like to share some true stories about the repercussions of not taking care of yourself or abusing your body that result in karmic lessons. One soul who came to me for counseling had hands that were severely crippled with arthritis. I learned that she liked to control everything; as a school principal, she lived in fear that if she could not control all outcomes, the school would end up failing and fall apart. She said that if that happened, she would see it as a personal failure. I explained to her the process of letting go and how to delegate authority to others. Then she could oversee those things without having direct control over them. After three weeks, the pain in her hands severely subsided and her hands became more flexible. One month later, however, she took back control of everything she had delegated; her hands once again became incapacitated.

I also had a female client who developed breast cancer. I helped her discover that a woman's breast is the giver of life to a woman's children because she uses it to feed them; it also is a reflection of how she is respected in life and honored in life as a female. I learned that this woman had gone through several marriages in which she was not loved or respected, and in some cases, physically abused. When she learned to let go of these emotions, she began to heal. Today, she remains cancer-free.

Another example of a karmic reaction is when males or females have reproductive problems or cancer because they are not respected as men or women, but instead, are abused and taken advantage of, whether physically, mentally, or emotionally. Those with back problems often have a karmic effect from carrying heavy financial or emotional loads on their bodies. When they understand and let go of those fears or emotions, no matter what they might be, their backs begin to heal. What I am trying to point out is that with the universal law of karma, for every action there is a reaction.

When I was living in Boston, I had some friends who had no place to live so I put them up at my house until they could get on their feet. Later, when I moved out to Washington State, I didn't know where I would live, but a friend from Boston had moved to Chehalis, Washington, so he invited me to stay with him. That is another example of karma. If nothing else, I hope you have learned in reading this chapter that karma is an experience, and as quickly as you understand what you are to learn from it, that karma will be over, along with the karmic debt. Karmic debt is merely an addendum to karma; it says that whatever you were to learn from some type of karma you created with someone or some situation, once it is learned is now paid back. An oversimplification of this is if you cheated someone in a past life, you would have to experience being cheated. Perhaps you stole some money from someone in a past life, and meeting that person in this lifetime, not knowing who the person is, you feel the inclination to assist him or her financially; doing so releases the karmic debt.

Since we create some type of karma in every lifetime, remember it is an experience that allows us to empower ourselves. Therefore, it is best for you to consider your actions in everything you do. By doing so, you will create a lesser impact in terms of the karma you need to experience in this lifetime as well as in future lifetimes. Remember, even if you give someone $1 million in this lifetime, it can create karma for you to come back and experience what it is to receive $1 million in another lifetime. Don't fear that because of karma you need to isolate yourself; instead, follow your heart and fully embrace it, experience it, and understand it. That will create a strong possibility that you will not have to come back to experience the same situations again, although that is not guaranteed.

Sometimes, our karma is intended to bring about change in this world, whether on a conscious, spiritual, human, or economic level. Many souls in both leadership and non-leadership roles are fulfilling their karma by bringing about positive changes. Some of these people could be considered religious leaders, spiritual leaders, world leaders, or everyday people who are helping each other make what we would consider minor changes, but which are truly monumental changes. An act of kindness, no matter who or where it comes from, creates a very positive karma by setting positive examples for others to follow. Through that act of kindness, you have changed the future of someone's life and his or her children and grandchildren's lives. What could be more powerful than that? Every day we go about changing everyone we meet, everything we see, and everything we do in a very positive way. One of my favorite quotes that I termed is (as relayed to me by God, the True Source):

> *"How others live life is their choice; how you live your life is your choice."*

Summary

In closing, it is important for you to remember that karma is nothing but an experience; it is neither positive nor negative, and it only exists to empower you and help you appreciate and enjoy life. I believe you will now understand that the Divine does not punish you, but rather, you create those experiences to grow and learn from. They are not punishments! They are only there for you to appreciate what you have created in the past and present and to understand how karma may affect your future.

EXERCISE

As usual, begin with the mantra of Dream Heaven. After you complete the mantra, answer the following questions.

First, make a list of everything presently occurring in your life, both positive and negative.

_____

_____

_____

_____

Ask what lessons and experiences you are to learn from the items on your list.

_____

_____

_____

_____

Meditate on what is needed for you to learn, heal, and release those karmic lessons. Write them down.

_____

_____

_____

_____

Before you ask for forgiveness of your karma and karmic debt, seek to feel the energy of the karma and karmic debt—to understand it, embrace it, and ask how you can be forgiven. Then make copious notes and follow through. This must be done with great sincerity; otherwise, you are only fooling yourself and creating more karma.

"Karma isn't revenge; it is a mirror of your soul's mistakes and for those who wish bad karma for you it is a mirror for their mistakes. Karma was never meant to be a punishment. It is a reminder of your soul's true self to be better than all the insecurities that hurt others because of your fear and lack in faith that God has a plan for you."

— Shannon L. Alder

CHAPTER 5

THE LAW OF ENLIGHTENMENT (SPIRITUAL PERFECTION)

"Within each of us is a light, awake, encoded in the fibers of our existence. Divine ecstasy is the total of this marvelous creation experienced in the hearts of humanity."

— Tony Samara

You have incarnated not only to experience life and karma, but to rediscover enlightenment in human form. This process allows you to heal all negative karma and negative karmic debt while at the same time changing your consciousness on the outer and inner plane of your existence. As you change your consciousness to enlightenment, your vibrations, frequencies, and energies touch all around you; this process opens up a door so others may also make the choice to raise their vibrations to choose enlightenment.

What is enlightenment? Well, it is easier to experience than to explain, but I will do my best. Enlightenment is not being controlled by other people's thoughts that are restrictive rules or judgments. It is freedom from anger, hate, insecurities, illness, materialism, frustration, and insecurities. It is the release of all controls that create fear. Being enlightened is to realize that you are not the slave of your fears and doubts. Rather, everything around you is merely an experience to observe, understand, and grow from. It is to understand by observation and compassion what others have chosen to constrict their growth and block their enlightenment, while not allowing yourself to be similarly imprisoned.

"If a man can control his mind, he will find the way to enlightenment. And all wisdom and virtue will naturally come to him."

— **Buddha**

Enlightenment is not composed of words, thoughts, nor things, but feelings of love, freedom, and joy with no strings attached. Enlightenment allows you to know that we are all individually a part of God, the True Source, and that in your life, you are choosing to experience those things that bring love, joy, and happiness. To be enlightened is to realize you are a divine aspect of God, the True Source, and that all of your needs will be satisfied on an unlimited basis as needed in order for you to obtain and feel complete and total freedom. The divine has related a wonderful mantra to me. I would like to share it with you: "I am of this planet, but not in the negative emotions of this planet."

We have incarnated not only to experience life and karma, but to rediscover enlightenment in human form. This process allows us to heal all negative karma and negative karmic debt while at the same time changing our consciousness from the outer (human) plane to the inner (spiritual) plane. As you begin to change your consciousness to enlightenment, a great and wonderful thing begins to occur. Your vibrations, frequencies, and energies rise to new levels, touching all around you and thus enabling others to open up themselves so they may make the choice of raising their vibrations to choose enlightenment. In essence, that means that each one of us is a catalyst of change to enlightenment for one another. The beauty within this process is that it takes no effort on your part to begin to change the world in the most positive way.

"You are destined for enlightenment. Cooperate with your destiny. Don't go against. Don't thwart it. Allow it to fulfill itself."

— **Nisargadatta Maharaj**

EXERCISE

As you begin to meditate, and before beginning your mantra of Dream Heaven, ask that God, the True Source, assist you in setting your ego aside.

Ask that your third eye be open, your chakras all be aligned in harmony along you're your polarities, and that your vibrations go to the highest level possible for you in order to begin the process of obtaining enlightenment. Then write down your experiences.

_____

_____

_____

_____

Ask that you now receive God, the True Source's unconditional love to fill every cell of your body. Write down what that feels like.

_____

_____

_____

_____

Begin to inhale "dream" and exhale "heaven." Have no expectations, and let the process begin. It is important that you do not give up and that you continue to do this process until you feel an acceleration of energy, deep unconditional love, and joy in your life.

SUMMARY

Remember that you are an important part of this universe and that by raising your vibrations and frequencies, you become enlightened. Your enlightenment, in turn, raises the vibrations and energies not only of yourself, but of everything around you, creating a far-reaching effect throughout our multi-dimensional universe on this planet and everywhere else. You become the pillar of change, which has the effect of the hundredth monkey syndrome. Congratulations! You are on your way.

CHAPTER 6

THE LAW OF NON-JUDGMENT

"If you concentrate on finding whatever is good in every situation, you will discover that your life will suddenly be filled with gratitude, a feeling that nurtures the soul."

— **Rabbi Harold Kushner**

There are three types of judgments: 1) self, 2) your perceptions, and 3) others' perceptions. All your perceptions and judgments come from either the influence of your parents, your religious background, and people you look up to or revere, or from anxiety, fear, insecurity, and your experiences.

We are always constantly making judgments of a personal nature based on others' influence by not fulfilling their expectations. Yet their expectations are merely judgments based upon their own perceptions and judgments fostered upon us. If you make others' judgments your reality, then you no longer grow, and you live in others' shadows. Think for a moment about Alexander Graham Bell believing in the telephone when others judged it was not possible, or perhaps Thomas Edison, who when a friend told him he had failed more than 1,000 times to develop the light bulb, replied that he had not failed but only learned what did not work. Neither of these great souls who changed the world let others' negative judgments influence them.

Every personal judgment you experience or inflict upon yourself is based in your own experiences, likes, and dislikes, and perhaps the influence and expectations of others. There are people who love spicy food, but if you have a sensitive stomach, you know that if you eat spicy foods, you will be uncomfortable. My point is that your personal judgments are for you and you alone, so apply them either positively or negatively to yourself.

"Do not judge so that you will not be judged."

— Jesus Christ

It is human nature to judge others based on our own opinions and experiences; however, in doing so, we are only making judgments about ourselves based on our own insecurities, blocks, or fears. What do we accomplish when we judge others? We only affirm what we want to believe rather than what is true. The problem with judging is that you judge and indict others based on what you righteously feel is correct. This begs the question, "What is correct?" Although there are certain truths that are undeniable— for example, "Thou shall not kill." The rest are merely opinions fostered by individuals or public sentiment. Most judgment comes from fear. When you judge others, you are judging yourself. This quote from the Ten Commandments is quite clear. However, it was later clarified in the Torah, the ancient history and teachings of rabbis, prophets, and other sages, that it was permissible to kill in certain situations; for example, when you need to defend your or your family members' lives or to protect your food source, etc. While one may interpret this to mean there are no absolutes, conditions and sound judgment apply.

"Our own worst enemy cannot harm us as much as our unwise thoughts. No one can help us as much as our own compassionate thoughts."

— Buddha

Each one of us has chosen the gift of life, which can be grand, joyful, and happy, or just the opposite—full of despair. It is important not to compare yourself to others but rather enjoy the life you have created and seek to expand that joy, for in the end, the only thing that counts is: How did you live life? What did you accomplish? What is your legacy? I wish you to know that it is important not to live in the shadow of others' opinions or belief systems, but rather, what is right action and what brings fulfillment to your life is not based in ego, materiality, and fear. The choice has always been yours, but through meditation and enlightenment, your soul and God, the True Source, will help you to achieve your mission and goal on the human and spiritual planes, which will bring you the greatest joy and love you have ever experienced.

"There's only one reason why you're not experiencing bliss at this present moment, and it's because you're thinking or focusing on what you don't have…. But, right now you have everything you need to be in bliss."

— Anthony de Mello

EXERCISE

Begin with Dream Heaven. During your meditation, ask the following questions. Afterwards, write down the answers you receive.

Of what am I judgmental?

_____

_____

_____

_____

Why is what I am judgmental of in my life? What is its purpose?

_____

_____

_____

_____

How may I see the truth and learn to become nonjudgmental?

_____

_____

_____

_____

In my conversations with God, the True Source, I have been reminded of the following: What was my truth at age twenty was no longer my truth at age thirty; what was my truth at thirty was no longer my truth at forty; what was my truth at forty was no longer my truth at fifty; and whatever was my truth at fifty was no longer my truth at sixty, and so on. Remember, everything in life is in a constant state of change, and you are part of that change, therefore you can decide whether it is negative or positive. The truth is that everything has always been your choice, and it shall always be so to the end of your days and into perpetuity.

Summary

You now realize that you can live your own life rather than trying to live up to the expectations of others. You have the freedom to be yourself, and to practice right action and correct exchange by now knowing you are perfect. Practicing right action and correct exchange frees you to be your true authentic self. With each experience, you grow into unlimited perfection. Remember, the definition of perfection means ever-growing more perfect. One of my favorite quotes that I termed is (as relayed to me by God, the True Source):

"To remain stagnant and stuck is to wither and die;
to grow and learn is to blossom and live."

CHAPTER 7

THE LAW OF PERFECT HEALTH

"The greatest wealth is health."

— Virgil

If we are to examine what God, the True Source, has created for us, then we realize that due to divine love, we are born perfect in each and every way. If the bearer of the fetus, the mother, takes reasonable care of herself, then the baby is born in perfect health; in some cases, if the mother does not take care of herself, the fetus may still be born healthy. All the perfect ingredients are combined together, like a cake made from scratch, to produce a perfect human being.

This miracle of life begs the question: What happens later in life to produce illness? The ability for the soul and body's energy to adapt is incredible if we merely get out of our own way, mentally and emotionally, and let our soul be guided by the Divine. That means that all outcomes will be perfect for each one of us. I have dealt with souls who are either born blind at birth or lose their sight later in life, and I have observed how quickly they adapt and become happy. We are all aware that blind people's other senses begin to expand, their intuition and awareness begins to increase, and they seem to be always protected. Even those with multiple sclerosis, muscular dystrophy, Lou Gehrig's disease, Parkinson's disease, and other illnesses learn how to adapt and take the challenge of converting lemons into lemonade.

Sometimes souls choose physical challenges as karmic lessons to heal and, at the same time, enjoy their lives. Whatever the lessons are, whether created at birth or later in life, it is important for us to know that it all has to do with our mind, emotions, spirit, and physical bodies.

"Every symptom has a story to tell about your life. A fascinating story, that can reveal the complex links between your body, mind, emotions and spirit."

— Kristina Turner

Understand that anything and everything that exists in our life is placed there for you to partake in for a reason—to create or enjoy happiness, joy, and perfect health. Joy and happiness are the main drugs for perfect health. We all know many people who complain about being victims and make every excuse for their physical and mental health. While their past life experiences as they describe them may be true, they have chosen, consciously or not, to let those experiences be excuses to paralyze them so they stay stuck in their pasts. What is necessary for you to realize is that every experience you have or have had is to empower you and help and allow you to heal those painful life experiences from your past. You must realize that you initially chose to experience or create those situations in order for your soul to grow and move forward and so you could achieve great healing and enlightenment. As soon as you allow the challenges of self-worth, self-esteem, and self-love to consume your life, they become the bars that keep you in prison, which leads to your physical, mental, emotional, energetic, and spiritual disintegration. That then morphs into the beginning phases of illnesses and diseases. If left unresolved, the situation may turn into a major block in your life.

Therefore, ask yourself, "How do I reverse these maladies?" First, it is important to realize that if this type of situation is occurring in your life, you have given up your self-empowerment and bought into futility and hopelessness. Realize that this situation is nothing more than an illusion created by despair; you have forgotten that you are divine and that at every level—physical, mental, emotional, energetic, cellular, vibrational frequency, life force energy, and total beingness—you are an aspect of God, the True Source. As you begin to recognize this truth and accept it fully, the healing process will begin.

If you would but stop to think as God, the True Source, the Alpha and Omega, and our Father and Mother, you will realize that since God, the True Source, has no illness and we are a divine aspect of it, then illness is something you have artificially created. If you believe that you have the unlimited power, ability, and energy, coupled with the desire, to be healed, then you will be healed. If you would but take a few moments to look back at the origins of your illness, realizing and understanding how you allowed it to take over your life, you can begin the process of releasing this negative energy in order to be healthy. First, you must ask yourself, "Why is this malady in my life? What is the *payoff* for me?" Understand that everything in your life, both negative and positive, you created for some specific reason. Obviously, if it is positive, you do not need to spend too much time on it, other than to realize how you created it; however, if it is not, then you must go through the painful process to discover the reason it is in your life. This is very important because what you discover and acknowledge is the beginning of the healing process that now begins to take place. Approximately 70 to 80 percent of healing takes place upon this realization; the remaining 20 to 30 percent is the part you have to work on in earnest to heal.

The next step necessary to heal is that you feel in-depth the emotion of how you created this malady to the depth of your very core. This is extremely important, and it may feel uncomfortable; however, the important part of this exercise is not to fool yourself that you have found the answer. Once the core issue has been discovered, felt, and experienced, it is now time to forgive yourself and turn it over to God, the True Source, to be cleansed, healed, and (most importantly), transmuted into perfect love on the outer plane, inner plane, and in your form.

The final step, which is just as important, is to ask that your body, at the deepest cellular, emotional, mental, and physical levels, be filled with God, the True Source's perfect unconditional love. All that is necessary now is for you to relax and let the healing begin. If this does not work immediately, by that I mean within fifteen to twenty minutes, repeat the process until you feel the release. If the release has not been experienced or felt, it is necessary to go back and repeat the process. After that has been completed, ask God, the True Source, that you now be healed of body, mind, and soul, spirit love and emotion, psyche, and every cell within and without in the outer plane, inner plane, and in your form. (Just a reminder: The outer plane is all that exists around you; the inner plane is the spiritual plane, and your form is your physical body.) If you find this difficult, do not beat yourself up; rather, realize what a brave soul you are to take on this perfect healing challenge.

"For health is not caused by something you don't have; it's caused by disturbing something you already have. Healthy is not something that you need to get; it's something you have already if you don't disturb it."

— **Dean Ornish**

Today, our life is filled with schedules, deadlines, stress, impatience, and self-imposed expectations, as well as expectations imposed on us by others. As a result, we do not stop to smell the flowers or take time to be at oneness and peace with our own individual selves. This situation creates disharmony in our spiritual, physical, emotional, and mental bodies, which, in turn, creates dis-ease. This dis-ease creates dis-harmony in our multidimensional bodies, which manifests itself in the outer form as a disease.

"The secret of health for both mind and body is not to mourn for the past, worry about the future, or anticipate troubles, but to live in the moment wisely and earnestly."

— **Buddha**

I have a client in her early twenties who has been blind since she was six years old. To go to work, she has to take a bus from a northern suburb of Seattle into Seattle and then another bus to get to work, and do it all over again in reverse to return home. She does this fearlessly with great ease and positive expectations. She is also contemplating going to college while working. There has never been a complaint uttered from her lips concerning her blindness. Another fine example was Dr. Stephen Hawking, reputed to have been the smartest man in the world. He went from having a normal body to being a complete paraplegic, but he did not complain; he just continued his work. I'm sure all of you reading this have many fine examples of others who have maladies that the average person would find devastating, and yet these souls manage to be positive role models to others and achieve greatness in their lives.

"Your body hears everything your mind says."

— Naomi Judd

EXERCISE

Proceed with the Dream Heaven exercise.

Begin your meditation and set the intention to know what needs to be healed and released. Write down the response you receive.

_____

_____

_____

_____

Now follow the process described in the chapter regarding what needs to be healed. Ask:

How did I create this situation in my life?

_____

_____

_____

_____

What am I to learn from this affliction?

_____

_____

_____

_____

What is the payoff for me?

_____

_____

_____

_____

After you discover this information, ask that you feel in-depth the emotion of how you created this malady to the depth of your very core. There may be some level of discomfort; however, that is a sign that you are on the right track. Once you find the core issue and experience it, it is time to forgive yourself and turn it over to God, the True Source, to be cleansed, healed, and most importantly, transmuted into perfect love on the outer plane, in the inner plane, and in your form.

Next, ask your body at the deepest cellular, emotional, mental, and physical levels to be filled with God, the True Source's perfect unconditional love.

If you have not felt the release, repeat the process until you do. If you find this difficult, just know that you are at the core issue, so by repeating this process, you will release it.

Once the process is completed, ask God, the True Source, to heal your body, mind, soul, spirit, love, motion, psyche, and every cell within on the outer plane, in the inner plane, and in your form. Congratulations! You have done a Herculean job of healing yourself.

SUMMARY

By now, you have discovered the secret to healing yourself, releasing your karma, and becoming your true authentic self as God, the True Source, desires you to be. Whenever you confront an obstacle in your life, you can return to the tools you learned in this chapter to restore your body and soul to equilibrium and perfect health. It is best to remember that you are Unlimited!

*"Healing comes when the individual remembers his or her identity—
the purpose chosen in the world of ancestral wisdom—
and reconnects with that world of spirit."*

— Malidoma Patrice Somé

CHAPTER 8

THE LAW OF PROSPERITY

"Prosperity is a state produced immediately by the mind. When the sun comes out of the clouds, everything is lit. When the mind comes out of duality, prosperity is there."

— Yogi Bhajan

What is duality? In essence, it is two opposing thoughts, and because those thoughts are opposed, they block your manifestation. For example, I desire unlimited prosperity in my life so that I may enjoy life, but at the same time, I may have the subconscious thought, "I am not worthy; I don't deserve it," or something else which is in complete opposition to what I am thinking and wanting to manifest. In essence, that is a duality.

How does one measure prosperity? Is prosperity perfect health? Is it joy? Is it happiness? Is it peace, harmony, and tranquility? Or is it just plain old-fashioned wealth. To some people in small, undeveloped countries, having food, shelter, and warmth each and every day is prosperity. To others, it is possessing huge sums of money and other material possessions. When we read books or watch movies depicting people who are extremely wealthy, we can develop mental blocks to our own prosperity by believing those people obtained it through luck, being born into wealth, or having some magical situation occur in their lives that can never happen to us. The truth is that those people created their own prosperity because they believed they could, and so they did, and so can you. Each person defines prosperity differently; however, in our society, it is defined as materialism and financial wealth. This definition is the cause of great anxiety, pain, and insecurity in our lives and societies. Our society has also created a belief in the haves and the have-nots. My mother used to say, "The rich get richer and the poor have children." If you believe in that, then that's all you'll manifest. If you believe that everything is possible and you are unlimited in what you can manifest and have, then you will also create whatever you think about. In essence, you are the creator of your prosperity or non-prosperity.

"Prosperity is the out-picturing of substance in our affairs. Everything in the universe is for us. Nothing is against us. Life is ever giving of itself. We must receive, utilize and extend the gift. Success and prosperity are spiritual attributes belonging to all people, but not necessarily used by all people."

— Ernest Holmes, *The Science of Mind*

Holmes's quote above verifies that everything is possible. Therefore, we need to explore what is blocking us from achieving prosperity. Most of our blocks comes from our parents and other authority figures' influence during our youth. We adopt and take ownership of their beliefs and negative words in our subconscious mind, which eventually causes them to manifest into our reality. For example, these people may have told you, "Money burns a hole in my pocket," "I will never have enough to obtain whatever I desire," "I have a few extra dollars in my bank account, but my car will probably break down and I'll have to use the money for that," "We grew up poor and that is our lot in life," "I never seem to get ahead," "We are outcasts from our family or society; therefore, we will never achieve success or great wealth," "I'm not worthy of prosperity because of some guilty family-influenced reason," "I am not good enough so I do not deserve prosperity," or "It is my punishment to be poor." I'm sure you've heard all these reasons and many more.

"Remember that money is the consolidation of the loving, living energy of divinity, and that the greater the realization and expression of love, the freer will be the inflow of that which is needed to carry forward the work."

— Djwhal Khul, Tibetan master

The reality is that as you think, so shall you create because that is the Law of Manifestation. You are divine, and you are a beautiful aspect of the Divine. Just as parents want the best for their children, so God, the True Source, wants the same for you. If you think about that for a few minutes, you will realize there is nothing in your life that you cannot have or achieve if you so desire it. To achieve whatever you want, you must have purity of thought, focus, and the knowingness that you are deserving; then it will soon arrive in your life. As I have said before, when you chose to incarnate, you knew your future lifestyle, parents, career, and even your missions and goals on the human plane and spiritual plane before that incarnation. You also knew just before your incarnation that whatever karmic lessons you would choose to learn could be healed quickly and that you could create a life of prosperity and abundance.

EXERCISE

Spend a moment contemplating the idea that "The ball is in your court." Then make a list of all the reasons you are not prosperous and abundant.

_____

_____

_____

_____

Make sure your list is as long as you can make it. Next, I would like you to look at all the reasons you have placed on this paper for why you are not prosperous and abundant and ask yourself "Why do I believe this reason?" for each one. Write down your answers.

_____

_____

_____

_____

Now make a list of twelve negative beliefs you have acquired in your youth and explain how they are blocking your prosperity.

_____

_____

_____

_____

_____

_____

_____

_____

_____

_____

_____

Next, make a list of twelve reasons why you deserve prosperity.

_____

_____

_____

_____

_____

_____

_____

_____

_____

_____

_____

Compare your list of reasons you are not prosperous and abundant with your list of why you deserve to be. Do you see any contradictions? Which reasons for why you're not prosperous and abundant can you cross off as not true?

_____

_____

_____

I strongly suggest at this point you begin the meditation of Dream Heaven with the 108 pennies.

When you have finished the meditation, review your lists again. Do you feel that the reasons you're not prosperous and abundant are nothing but illusions you have created in your life or based in some belief system that is no longer valid? Do you believe you are now at a place where you can attract unlimited prosperity and abundance? If you have not fully embraced that you are deserving, repeat the mantra of Dream Heaven once again, only this time, instead of inhaling "dream" and exhaling "heaven," inhale "I am" and exhale "prosperous!" Remember, all thoughts are electromagnetic, so what you are creating is a vibration and frequency to create prosperity into your life. By using the words "I am," you are affirming that you are one with the Divine, the Divine is one with you, and you are both co-creating unlimited prosperity into your life. This affirmation of prosperity and abundance does not judge whether or not you are worthy; it simply manifests into your life based upon your thoughts. It is also important to remember that all thoughts are created into your life based on your belief system. Sometimes you will find that you will have to do this affirmation consistently a couple of times a day until the manifestation is created in your life, not because you're unworthy, but because you doubt it. As you create this knowingness that you are worthy, you will create a vibrational stream of prosperity in your life for perpetuity.

Make a list of at least three reasons you deserve unlimited prosperity now.

_____

_____

_____

*"If you feel just one thing in your life—that life is nothing but
the gift of God—you are divine and the most courageous person.
Try it! Try it as a thought. The moment you feel that life
is a gift, you'll become prosperous."*

— Yogi Bhajan

SUMMARY

Your attitude, feelings, emotions, and thoughts all determine
whether you have unlimited prosperity and abundance. John
Randolph Price calls money, "my own natural energy yield." The yield
is the effect or the outer symbol of the inner supply while the cause is
your God-given essence—the energy that underlies the outer manifestation. Think of it this way: The spiritual definition of money is both
cause and effect, both visible and invisible, both consciousness and
form, both giver and gift. In essence, Price is saying, "Do not focus on
the form of money as your supply, but rather recognize the energy of
money. Our spiritual consciousness can create the manifestation that
will let the form, money, appear. Once you realize you are worthy
of unlimited prosperity and abundance, hold on to that thought
and know that all doors are now opening for you to achieve it at the
proper time. The proper time is always God, the True Source's perfect
timing for you. You will be clearly led to opportunities to achieve it.
Remember, you are divine; you are an aspect of God, the True Source.
God, the True Source, wants and desires everything that brings joy
and happiness into your life. Never doubt this; never question it, and
know that it is an immutable truth. One of my favorite quotes that I
termed is (as relayed to me by God, the True Source):

*"All life is an illusion. You are the 'soul' creator of your life;
as you think and believe, it becomes."*

CHAPTER 9

THE LAW OF GRATITUDE

"It [gratitude] turns what we have into enough, and more. It turns denial into acceptance, chaos into order, confusion into clarity.... Gratitude makes sense of our past, brings peace for today, and creates a vision for tomorrow."

— Melody Beattie

In today's world, we very seldom hear the words "Thank you." Rather than gratitude, I see around us greed, dissatisfaction, anger, frustration, and self-imposed victimization. When you live your life in those modes, all you are expressing, indirectly, is ingratitude for your situation. You may not realize it, but whatever you are expressing to the universe, you are creating in your life. I've met some who revel in the joy of victimization, in being in a state of lack, in being poor, or in many other negative situations because for them such states are an excuse and perhaps a badge of honor. I hear some psychologists and psychiatrists say it is not our children or other souls' faults when they are in bad situations because they are victims. Wow, what a way to place a person in a prison from which he can now have an excuse for his situation and actions and not have to be responsible.

I also hear constant complaints from parents and grandparents, who tell me that when they give gifts to their children or grandchildren, they very seldom receive a thank you. I also hear complaints from those who have attended weddings and brought gifts that they do not receive back thank you notes. When I've held dinner parties, very seldom have I heard "Thank you" or "The dinner was great" at the end of the evening. It used to be a custom that whenever you went to someone's house for dinner, not only did you thank your host, but also, if it was the first time you had been invited, you also sent a thank you note. You always brought a gift to the host/hostess to demonstrate appreciation. Growing up, I remember my parents telling me always to say thank you when a gift was given to me, even if I didn't like it. There was greater wisdom in saying thank you than I realized at that time. But now when I look at the universal laws and especially the Law of Gratitude, I see the wisdom in saying thank you.

The universe responds to our words and thoughts without determining whether they are positive or negative. As I pointed out earlier, electricity is neutral energy that can power a house or a train or can cause great destruction through fire or electrocution. Electricity does not determine how it is to be used; we determine that. The same applies to gratitude. Whenever you express it, it is drawn into your life even if it is in the negative form of ingratitude. If you understand this simple concept, then you realize you are responsible for every joy, happiness, and positive thing that occurs in your life as well as those that are negative and unpleasant.

"Gratitude is the great attitude."

— Author Unknown

In my classes, I've often taught that every time you pay a bill, whether online, via check, or in person, you always give thanks for the prosperity and abundance you have that gives you the opportunity to pay the bill. Do not discriminate whether you are paying it partially or in full; either way, it behooves you to give thanks. When someone gives you a gift, you give thanks. When someone goes out of her way to assist you, give thanks. It's interesting how so many people today have forgotten to do that and do not go out of their way if it is inconvenient and there is no payoff for them. In truth, there is a payoff for every time you show gratitude and say thank you. For, you see, according to the Law of Electromagnetic Attraction, whatever you express to the universe, whether positive or negative, in the form of gratitude or ingratitude, the universe will respond by saying, "Oh, you must like this so we should give you more." If you are expressing fear, doubt, negativity, anxiety, or hate, that is what you will draw into your life. If you are expressing gratitude for the love, joy, prosperity, and abundance in your life, you will continue to attract them. It is so overly simple and yet so complex that many souls do not understand the basic principles of the universe and divine love. Expressing gratitude is a form of love!

"Be thankful for what you have; you'll end up having more. If you concentrate on what you don't have, you will never, ever have enough."

— Oprah Winfrey

God, the True Source, has told me we can change a person's life by expressing a form of gratitude. For example, if I go into a store and see someone who is tired or looking glum, I can give that person a compliment. Instantly, his whole face will begin to glow, he will have a new liveliness in his step, and his personality will change. Then I have the satisfaction of having changed that person's day to one of joy and appreciation. This is so simple to do, yet I notice when I go shopping or am in a medical office that instead, people complain, scream, and yell. I was taught growing up that you always get more with honey than vinegar, and I take that even further by expressing gratitude.

On a personal level, I teach the students in my classes to give thanks to anyone who has ever bought them breakfast, lunch, or dinner, and I ask that they say this three times a day. The net result is that in two weeks or less, someone will invite that person out for breakfast, lunch, or dinner. This is an example of how gratitude manifests in our lives. One of my basic requirements in the classes I teach is that we are to make a difference each and every day in the lives of those around us. I so enjoy listening to my students later share their experiences of how they made people's faces light up and how those people became joyous and happy.

"At times our own light goes out and is rekindled by a spark from another person. Each of us has cause to think with deep gratitude of those who have lighted the flame within us."

— Albert Schweitzer

EXERCISE

Begin your meditation of Dream Heaven.

Make a list of all the negative things you have recently expressed, such as fear, anger, or disgust.

_____

_____

_____

_____

_____

_____

_____

_____

Review your list to determine how you can show gratitude for what you perceive as negative things in your life.

_____

_____

_____

_____

_____

_____

_____

Make another list of all the things that you can express positive gratitude for in your life.

_____

_____

_____

_____

_____

_____

_____

_____

Add to this list those positive, empowering things you desire to manifest into your life.

_____

_____

_____

_____

_____

_____

_____

Think about how you can make a difference with your friends, family, relatives, and coworkers.

_____

_____

_____

_____

_____

_____

_____

Think about how you can make a difference not only in your life but in someone else's.

Practice gratitude and making a difference in others' lives each and every day until it becomes second nature.

It is important to remember that nothing in this universe is fixed; each day brings a new experience that gives you the opportunity to learn and grow. Each moment is an expression of our thoughts, and we now know we can channel those thoughts to create all the things in our lives that bring about great gratitude. As you begin to contemplate this truth even more, you will realize that you are the sole (soul) creator of all your experiences; if these experiences have been negative in your thinking, give thanks for them because they are still empowering. For example, if you had not burned your finger on something hot, you would not have learned what hot is, so give thanks for that experience because now you are better able to protect yourself. Everything that occurs in your life is empowering, even the darkest and most negative experiences you can imagine. It is best for you to understand that every experience you have is an expression of learning and growing, both on the human and soul levels.

"I truly believe we can either see the connections, celebrate them, and express gratitude for our blessings, or we can see life as a string of coincidences that have no meaning or connection. For me, I'm going to believe in miracles, celebrate life, rejoice in the views of eternity, and hope my choices will create a positive ripple effect in the lives of others. This is my choice."

— Mike Ericksen

SUMMARY

It is important not only that we express gratitude and show appreciation, but that we also model them for others so they will finally understand and also come to live the universal Law of Gratitude. Make a concerted effort to model gratitude and be amazed by the results you experience.

"As we express our gratitude, we must never forget that the highest appreciation is not to utter words, but to live by them."

— John F. Kennedy

CHAPTER 10

THE LAW OF SURRENDER

"Something amazing happens when we surrender and just love.
We melt into another world, a realm of power already within us.
The world changes when we change. The world softens when we soften.
The world loves us when we choose to love the world."

— **Marianne Williamson**

We all know people around us who are controllers and manipulators. Have you ever stopped to ask yourself why they are that way and why they are in your life? Basically, controllers and manipulators are fearful of outcomes that are negative or contrary to what they desire. Sooner or later, they end up failing and paying a very difficult price for their attempts to control and manipulate. Obviously, those who follow these practices are fear-based. In some cases, they have learned these behaviors from past experiences or their family environment. In other cases, they acquire these behaviors because of a deep-seated event that occurred in their lives or from the fear that it will occur. These poor souls seek power for recognition, financial gain, and to have their egos stroked because they are so full of fear, doubt, insecurity, and low self-esteem that such behavior is the only way they can feel worthwhile. We have all experienced having these types of people in our personal, work, and even spiritual lives. These souls are afraid to say, "I don't know." They would figuratively go down with the ship just to prove a point, even if it causes their demise.

"As long as we have practiced neither concentration nor mindfulness,
the ego takes itself for granted and remains its usual normal size,
as big as the people around one will allow."

— Ayya Khema

Prior to your current incarnation, you chose a life that would bring about various experiences that would heal your karma and/or karmic debt; then you would be able to create situations to empower yourself to achieve your missions and goals on the human and spiritual planes. If you spend your time always living in fear because of your past and trying to control or manipulate certain outcomes in your future, you are only fooling yourself. All you achieve by following the path of control and manipulation is a life that is incomplete and full of fear, anger, frustration, insecurity, and anxiety. Your manipulative and controlling behaviors create negative energy that will wear down your physical body and create illness in it. The negative energy will also create chaos at all levels of your life. I have witnessed many controllers and manipulators who have developed arthritis in their hands, knees, feet, and elsewhere because they held on too tightly to their attempts to control everything. When I worked with them and taught them the process of letting go of their need to control, they discovered that their arthritic symptoms were beginning to decrease to the extent that they could again function normally. Those who followed my suggestion and practices for letting go achieved great success, while those who went back to their old ways found that they were once again crippled by the need to manipulate and/or control.

"By breaking down our sense of self-importance, all we lose is a parasite that has long infected our minds. What we gain in return is freedom, openness of mind, spontaneity, simplicity, altruism: all qualities inherent in happiness."

— Matthieu Ricard

Your life is all about trust, joy, love, and being in the flow with everything that occurs in, around, and about you. What is it in you that creates the desire and the will to be out of the flow of God, the True Source's love, harmony, and all that brings you joy in your life, including but not limited to love, perfect health, prosperity, abundance, positive spiritual empowerment, and enlightenment? It is important for you to realize that you asked for all of these experiences before you incarnated. The object of these experiences was for you to understand your place in the universe and how beautiful, wonderful, and loving God, the True Source, has always been.

"In the end these things matter most: How well did you love? How fully did you love? How deeply did you learn to let go?"

— Buddha

EXERCISE

Begin the mantra of Dream Heaven. As you meditate, ask your-self the following questions and write down the answers you receive.

What in my life am I trying to control and why?

_____

_____

_____

_____

_____

_____

_____

_____

What benefits am I obtaining from controlling?

_____

_____

_____

_____

_____

_____

_____

If I let go of control, what am I afraid will happen?

_____

_____

_____

_____
_____
_____
_____

What am I missing out on by having tunnel vision?

_____
_____
_____
_____
_____
_____
_____
_____

Where did I learn how to be a controller?

_____
_____
_____
_____
_____
_____
_____

What can I not let go of?

_____
_____
_____

_____

_____

_____

_____

_____

If I decide to change and let go, what are the unlimited possibilities for me?

_____

_____

_____

_____

_____

_____

_____

_____

Once you have all the information you have received in your meditations, ask God, the True Source, to help you heal and release your need for control with love, joy, grace, harmony, balance, ease, protection, perfection, and assistance at all levels, on the outer plane, in the inner plane, and in your form.

Many of my clients who were stuck in the past used the excuse that they were victims for why their lives were so tumultuous. Some of them would have figuratively and literally gone down with the ship, denying the ship was sinking, just to hang on to this belief.

The truth is that every experience we have is a gift. You only need to change your thinking three degrees to begin to enjoy life. If you're unhappy, you're at -1°. Try to move to a neutral 0° and then a

+1° as you focus on the changes you are beginning to make in your life. If you comprehend that everything you experience is a gift to empower you, help you gain knowledge, and begin to heal some past or current life karma and karmic debt, and if you are willing to do so, then you will realize that you have freed yourself from the shackles of the illusion that you are in prison. This prison is something you have created so you could stay stuck because your ego, pride, self-worth, or self-esteem has been seriously injured. Your prison has become comfortable; however, changing it can seem scary. But letting go and realizing that every experience, although it may be painful, is empowering and will free you not only in this lifetime but in future lifetimes, will allow you to enjoy life once again. One reason you incarnated was to experience the feeling of empowerment when you free yourself from these chains.

I have a wonderful client who has been married three times, and each marriage turned out to be a disaster. In fact, in the last marriage, she was severely physically abused. She ended up having no money, being unable to get Medicaid, Social Security, or any other kind of assistance, and having to sleep in her car for almost a year and a half. She was rejected by her family as well. Finally, after finding an attorney, she was able to get Medicaid and Social Security assistance. Today, she lives in a pleasant apartment but has to live frugally in order to pay her rent.

One day as we were having a conversation, this client told me she had a pretty good life. She felt that everything she had gone through had given her strength and encouraged her to continue with her life. She looked upon all of her experiences as an empowering gift and healing from past lives. What a wonderful soul to express those experiences to me. How powerful she was to realize these experiences were only a phase in her life and that when one door closed, another door would open. She knew that someday things would become even more joyous and happy for her.

SUMMARY

Many souls like to lay guilt trips on their family members or seek gratification or some type of excuse for their experiences; yet the true soul will regard these experiences as learning lessons, understanding that control and manipulation lead to more control and manipulation and, eventually, a dead-end. I remind you once again that God, the True Source, desires everything for you that will bring you joy and happiness. What greater gift could you ask for from the Divine than joy and happiness? When I have expressed this wisdom to my clients, some have only understood about joy and happiness but did not equate the benefits with prosperity, abundance, or perfect health. They were disappointed that it did not include the latter. That is because they had blinders on and could not see the forest for the trees. I had to remind them that everything—everything—that brings you joy and happiness to complete your life is now available for you when you surrender and let go of the need to control situations and those around you. It is our human nature to fear letting go because you fear the outcome will result in failure. However, that fear and need to control will only result in the failure you want to avoid because you are focused on failure and, consequently, attract it.

It comes down to a trust issue. Once you turn over everything to the Divine and truly realize you are unconditionally loved by God, the True Source, everything you desire will manifest for you without limitations. It is then, and only then, that you will see those positive changes occurring in your life. You need to let go and surrender right away. You have wasted enough time living in misery by trying to control a situation or believing it is impossible to change it. Now is the time to let it go. The limitations you know are only imaginary and self-created in your mind. Dismiss them. Remember, you are the sole (soul) creator of your life. *Surrender, let go, and let God, the True Source!*

"We are at our most powerful the moment we no longer need to be powerful."

— Eric Micha'el Leventhal

CHAPTER 11

THE LAW OF PERFECTION

"We have the need to be accepted and to be loved by others, but we cannot accept and love ourselves. The more self-love we have, the less we will experience self-abuse. Self-abuse comes from self-rejection, and self-rejection comes from having an image of what it means to be perfect and never measuring up to that ideal. Our image of perfection is the reason we reject ourselves; it is why we don't accept ourselves the way we are, and why we don't accept others the way they are."

— Miguel Angel Ruiz

An old cliché says, "Beauty is in the eye of the beholder." The challenge is that everyone's definition of beauty is different, and there's a fine line between beauty and perfection. In most instances, they are the same. As I look around, I see so many people watching the Academy Awards on TV and then going out to buy articles of clothing like the movie stars wore on the red carpet. They purchase these items because they believe they will make them look more pleasantly attired, beautiful, desirable, and perfect.

I have had male and female clients who have had to buy the latest clothing, footwear, jewelry, vehicles, furniture, housing, boats, and other accoutrements. By doing so, they wish to make the statement, "I have arrived" or "Look at me; I am perfect because I am successful." Or perhaps they have to have lavish parties, with expensive gourmet foods, and famous entertainers. All this means is, "I enjoy being stroked, admired, and worshiped for being perfect in each and every way."

Such people may also have their bodies altered with facelifts and other cosmetic surgeries to make themselves more youthful, desirable, and perfect. However, as a minister, I have presided over the marriages of 400-pound men to 110-pound women and vice versa. In these cases, each saw the perfection in the other and the beauty within.

In some cultures, being thin and other physical attributes are viewed as more attractive and desirable. In other cultures, if a person is fat, heavy, or perhaps just more voluptuous, he or she is seen as more desirable. Some cultures revere blond, red, auburn, brown, black, or multicolored hair. Some people appear beautiful to some and distasteful to others—take overly muscular bodybuilders as an example, or anorexic models. When I walk down the streets of a major city, I see all kinds of people dressed in all types of clothing. Whether I consider their clothing choices tasteful or not, each one believes he or she looks perfect. The truth is that each person has his or her own definition of looking perfect.

I prefer, as the quote by Steve Maraboli below illustrates, to think that we are all perfectly imperfect, and we learn much more from our imperfections. Steve writes:

> We have all heard that no two snowflakes are alike. Each snowflake takes the perfect form for the maximum efficiency and

effectiveness for its journey. And while the universal force of gravity is a shared destination, the expansive space in the air gives each snowflake the opportunity to take their own path. Along this gravity-driven journey, some snowflakes collide and damage each other, others collide and join together, some are influenced by the wind.... There are so many transitions and changes that take place along the journey of the snowflake. But no matter what the transition, the snowflake always finds itself perfectly shaped for its journey. I find parallels in nature to be a beautiful reflection of grand orchestration. One of these parallels is of the snowflake and us. We, too, are all headed in the same direction. We are driven by a universal force to the same direction. We are all individuals taking different journeys in a long journey, we sometimes bump into each other, we cross paths, we become altered.... We take different physical forms. But at all times we are 100 percent perfectly imperfect. At every given moment we are absolutely perfect for what is required for our journey. I'm not perfect for your journey and you're not perfect for my journey, but I'm perfect for my journey and you're perfect for your journey. We're heading to the same place, or taking different routes that were both exactly perfect the way we are. Think of what understanding this great orchestration could mean for relationships. Imagine interacting with others knowing that they too each share this parallel with the snowflake. Like you, they are headed to the same place and no matter what they may appear like to you, they have taken the perfect forms for their journey. How strong our relationships would be if we could see and respect that we are all perfectly imperfect for our journey.

The truth is that whatever we wear or whatever our definition is of perfection, it is not about what we are wearing or owning or what other material things we may have; it is all about attempting to be accepted by others. The fallacy in this thinking is that each person's definition of perfection is unique and different. I praise the person who dresses in the attire she feels in the mood to wear, or who drives the car that makes him feel comfortable, or who buys jewelry, footwear, or a home that makes him or her feel comfortable. Our society is so inured to the need to be accepted that too many people have not found what truly makes them happy. The challenge with trying to be perfect is you have to keep raising the bar to keep up with society and feel accepted. In striving for perfection, you spend more time looking at your imperfections. Wouldn't it feel better to look at the beauty within you, which isn't exterior but better represents who and what you are? The focus should be on your essence, the love and beauty within you. As it says in the Bible, we are made in the image of God, the True Source. Think about that for a moment; is not God, the True Source, perfect in each and every way? That is the essence of the Divine, so, without a doubt, it is our essence. It is only our fear of not living up to society's expectations that makes you consider yourself imperfect.

"Mindful and creative, a child who has neither a path,
nor examples to follow, nor value judgments, simply lives,
speaks and plays in freedom."

— **Arnaud Desjardins**

EXERCISE

Begin the mantra of Dream Heaven 108 times.

Make a list below of what you believe are five of your imperfections.

_____

_____

_____

_____

_____

Why do you have this belief system that you are imperfect?

_____

_____

_____

_____

_____

Which of these five imperfections stands out the most in your mind, and how does it apply to your life?

_____

_____

_____

_____

_____

How could you change your life to make yourself a better mother, father, daughter, son, parent, friend, coworker, etc.? List five answers below.

_____

_____

_____

_____

_____

If you could make these hypothetical changes, would that change your true essence?

_____

_____

_____

_____

_____

If making these changes were a lifetime endeavor, how would it change you in the last days of your life?

_____

_____

_____

_____

_____

What are five important things you wish to accomplish in your life?

_____

_____

_____

_____

_____

Finally, consider this: If you could have these things accomplished by the end of your life, would you not have achieved perfection in these accomplishments?

"For everything in this journey of life we are on, there is a right wing and a left wing: for the wing of love there is anger; for the wing of destiny there is fear; for the wing of pain there is healing; for the wing of hurt there is forgiveness; for the wing of pride there is humility; for the wing of giving there is taking; for the wing of tears there is joy; for the wing of rejection there is acceptance; for the wing of judgment there is grace; for the wing of honor there is shame; for the wing of letting go there is the wing of keeping. We can only fly with two wings and two wings can only stay in the air if there is a balance. Two beautiful wings is perfection. There is a generation of people who idealize perfection as the existence of only one of these wings every time. But I see that a bird with one wing is imperfect. An angel with one wing is imperfect. A butterfly with one wing is dead. So this generation of people strive to always cut off the other wing in the hopes of embodying their ideal of perfection, and in doing so, have created a crippled race."

— C. JoyBell C.

Summary

Our thoughts are a reflection of our bodies. The cellular structure of your body has an intelligence of its own and thinks in only "black and white" without any middle ground. Therefore, whatever you see as an imperfection of yourself—physically, mentally, or emotionally—your body will reflect. This is the opposite of what you are trying to achieve according to your personal definition of perfection. If you look in the mirror and see that you are not the right body shape, or your skin is not vibrant, or your hair is not perfect by your definition, or you are growing old, or whatever imperfection you see, you will become that/those imperfections. That is the Law of Manifestation: Whatever you think will manifest into your life.

Take time to understand the various spiritual laws and how they have all tied together to create what you have now become. Particularly examine the Law of Manifestation, the Law of Opposites, and the Law of Love; then you will understand what you have created. When we see imperfections in others, we are really seeing those imperfections in ourselves, whether they are real or hypothetical and based in fear. Remember that you asked for life so you could experience it in all its glory. Along the way you have made decisions based on your insecurities. I would suggest that you look at those insecurities and imperfections as an opportunity to experience your lack of love for yourself and to realize how beautiful and perfect you are.

Once when I was talking to God, the True Source, about perfection, I was told to go outside and look at a rosebush that was at least forty years old. God, the True Source, then asked me, "Do the red roses look brighter this year?" I replied, "I believe they do." Next, I was asked, "Are the flowers more fragrant this year?" It was easy for me to answer yes because I could smell the sweetness of the roses from several feet away. Next, I was asked, "Did you not think the roses were beautiful last year?" I had and I remembered admiring them, but I had to agree that they seemed bigger, brighter, and more fragrant this year. That's when I understood the definition of perfection. The rosebush believed itself to be perfect last year, and that thought of perfection in its energy field caused it to become even more perfect this year. In essence, perfection means ever-growing more perfect. In other words, we never achieve perfection because it is an ongoing process. Something may seem perfect, but then ways are found to improve upon it. How many times have we seen a little baby who was average-looking but grew up to be handsome or beautiful? The baby was perfect when born, but it is continuing to become more perfect, more handsome, and more beautiful. The same is true of you—you are ever-growing more perfect.

Each night before you go to sleep, look at your reflection in the mirror, and affirm with love and joy that you are perfect and ever-growing more perfect. Repeat this affirmation seven times with passion and belief. Do it for a minimum of sixty days. Then watch the magic begin.

"Contentment is a state of grace, a state of peace and happiness, appreciation and enjoyment for what it is, right now. Desires, in contrast, can never be satisfied. Once we get what we crave, we soon will find it less satisfying than we expected, so we strive for something else. The only escape from this perpetual wheel of want is to discover the contentment and perfection we already have."

— **Gillian Stokes**

CHAPTER 12

THE LAW OF COMPASSIONATE UNDERSTANDING AND FORGIVENESS

"A human being is part of the whole, called by us 'universe,' limited in time and space. He experiences himself, his thoughts and feelings as something separated from the rest—a kind of optical delusion of his consciousness. This delusion is a prison, restricting us to our personal desires and to affection for a few persons close to us. Our task must be to free ourselves from our prison by widening our circle of compassion to embrace all humanity and the whole of nature in its beauty."

— **Albert Einstein**

What is compassion, understanding, and forgiveness? It is a selfless act of realizing that your soul is going through some type of agony, pain, insecurity, fear, or anxiety not fully understood or embraced. It is understanding that the soul was so fully immersed in those emotions that it could not understand why those emotions were occurring in your life; at the same time, you were a prisoner of those emotions. The observer might only see pain and frustration, but you, experiencing those emotions, feel unloved, unwanted, misunderstood, and alone. You feel like you are out on the ocean with no lifejacket, no lifeboat, and totally abandoned.

An old Native American saying, "Never judge a person until you have walked a mile in his moccasins" reminds us that none of us can see or fully understand what another soul is experiencing. As a result, we must show compassion and love whenever we meet anyone. Sometimes that compassion and love can take on the form of simply opening a door for someone—metaphorically, that door could be the difference between that person walking in darkness or light. The proverb, "Feed a man a fish and he eats for a day; teach a man to fish and he eats every day," also reflects the value of compassionate understanding and how compassion can lead to empowerment for the person receiving it.

A fine line exists between compassionate understanding and forgiveness, yet many times, they are one and the same. The act of compassionate understanding then becomes an act of forgiveness as well.

I once helped a close friend through a divorce. When this person later became involved in another relationship, he often called me and I would go over to his house late at night to help him and his significant other through the emotional difficulties they were having with each other. At the same time, this person was trying to obtain disability from the military. I wrote a twenty-page report for him that assisted him in getting disability. As a minister, I married him and his girlfriend, gratis, and gave him a cash gift as well. This particular person was not only a great friend, but he and his wife were students in my classes. Because he was having financial challenges, I also reduced the class fees. You would think he would be grateful to me for all I had done.

Then one evening while I was teaching a class, he told me he had been reading a book that talked about manifestation. He then decided that the reason he could not manifest abundance in his life was because in teaching how to do so, I had left out one word. He started to yell at me and turned ashen gray. That's when I realized something had taken him over. I asked him to calm down. It took him some time to calm down, but he did so. Shortly thereafter, he decided, after rereading the book, that he would quit the class. His wife desired to support him so she also dropped out of class. At first, I was deeply hurt because we had been friends and he had been a student for over ten years, but then I realized that perhaps he could not grasp the big picture. These fears concerning prosperity were greater than him! According to the Law of Attraction, everything must be done with great intent and positive expectations, knowing the desired outcome will occur.

I did not speak to him for several years until I happened to be at a psychic fair where I saw him with his wife. Then I heard God, the True Source, talk to me about a class I had taught on compassion, understanding, and forgiveness. So, I went over to his area and gave him and his wife a big hug. Later, I proceeded to help them pack up when the psychic fair was over. I'm sure he felt a big relief as did I. I not only practiced but exhibited compassionate love and understanding.

Sometimes, compassion can take on the form of just listening. Many times, I've found that by listening to a person and asking only a very few short questions, the person can come to a greater understanding and begin the process of resolving his or her issues. Too often, however, our human consciousness is quick to judge, offer a solution, or give unwanted advice. We want to be rescuers because we arrogantly think we have all the answers without knowing, in detail, what that soul is going through. Usually, all the person desires is just to be heard. We must understand that we cannot heal or resolve another person's problems; in truth, individuals can only heal themselves. If, by chance, we choose to assist them by doing their work for them, we become enablers. Our payoff then is that we feel we have done a good service so we can pat ourselves on the back. In truth, we have not let them learn anything, so when a similar situation arises, they are stuck once again.

When we choose compassionate understanding and forgiveness, we perform a great healing not only for those involved, but more importantly, for ourselves. It is important to realize that frustration and anger cause disharmony in our energy fields, which ultimately causes more anger and frustration, plus insecurities, lack of self-worth, lack of self-love, and all other types of emotions that eventually surface into our bodies as some type of illness. Most of the time, these illnesses are like hot lava in a volcano waiting to erupt. The moral here is that the more we express compassion, understanding, and forgiveness, the more we heal and grow emotionally and spiritually. This healing and growth will occur for you whether or not the person accepts the compassion, understanding, and healing. Remember, it is up to that person whether to accept compassionate understanding and heal.

Compassionate understanding and forgiveness are a vibration frequency that allows each one of us individually to heal physically, mentally, emotionally, and spiritually. How many families do we look at that are at odds with one another? They are always complaining, expressing negativity, and being upset with each other. They are constantly needing to be validated for their negative behavior. I find it fascinating that the human race finds it so easy to believe something negative about a situation, person, or place. The huge majority of the time, no one makes the effort to substantiate that negative story or comment about a situation or person. What does that say about each one of us as part of the human race? Are we naïvely insecure, or are we just too involved in a soap opera?

Today, the media bombards us with negative stories. There used to be a saying in the news business, "If it bleeds, it leads." The world today is divided, politically and emotionally. There seem to be some forces out there that fan the fires of insecurity and discontent. We have become so focused on materiality that we have forgotten the very basics of life and our spiritual heritage. This is nothing new; it has been going on since humanity began. One of the very basic needs of life (unconditional love and nonjudgmentalness) appears to be forgotten or tossed aside because it does not fit into our world today. Those who practice it are either laughed at or taken advantage of; however, they are the true enlightened souls, free of shackles and chains of life.

> *"The chemist who can extract from his heart's elements compassion, respect, longing, patience, regret, surprise, and forgiveness and compound them into one can create the atom which is called love."*
>
> **— Kahlil Gibran**

THE STEPS OF FORGIVENESS

Step One: Release the Pain of the Past.

There are many definitions of forgiveness. Perhaps the best one to look at is the meaning of forgiveness: it is to finish, allowing the pain of the past to be released so we can move on to focus on a positive future. This allows you to leave the pain of the past with others who have created it or allowed it to be created in your life. All the pain, anxiety, and frustrations you have created in your life, whether from situations, persons, or conditions, have placed barriers in your life that paralyze your physical, mental, and spiritual growth. As a result, you are tied to a chain of anger and fear that handicaps you from achievement. It limits your ability to follow your true spiritual path, your mission, and your goals. It creates anger and fear. Fear is anger expressed, and anger is fear repressed.

It is important to recognize the origin of the mental and or emotional pain in your life. Accept the fact that you have allowed this pain into your life for a specific reason. You are not a victim! It is important to examine thoroughly the reason it has come into your life by paying attention to how you feel; then look at it figuratively, from the perspective of the perpetrator of that incident. Finally, look at it from an observer's perspective, seeing it from all angles with no judgment.

Step Two: Understand What the Pain Is Meant to Teach You.

It is important to realize that you need to dig deep into your heart and consciousness to release the pain and uproot this emotion; realize that the pain in your heart and body was created for a reason: to empower you. But you can have more power when you learn not to control nor express your opinions to others, but rather to let everyone decide on his or her own individual path and what he or she desires to learn. Whether you judge what others do as right or wrong is immaterial. Each individual has his or her own path of forgiveness, which it is not necessary for you to understand; we need to let go and let God, the True Source, take charge and realize that everything that occurs in someone else's life is for understanding, knowledge, and personal growth. Many times when you are wrong, your ego, emotions, self-worth, self-esteem, or pride is injured. In doing so, you become stubborn and refuse to look at whatever created this frustration and anger in your life, not truly understanding why you drew it into your life. Once you dig deep and find that you understand what it is all about, you begin the process of healing by releasing and thus moving forward.

Now is the time to comprehend fully what you are to learn. As I said before, this pain occurred in your life to heal and empower you. There are no victims! After you fully understand the lesson to be learned, you have now opened the door to unlimited healing.

Step Three: Forgive Yourself.

Why forgive? Because when you forgive, you forgive your own personal pain. Without forgiveness, all your feelings of insecurity, anger, frustration, unworthiness, and not being appreciated, recognized, or respected become a poison in your body. Sooner or later, those feelings manifest into high blood pressure, ulcers, cancer, or other debilitating illnesses. One of the most transparent of these illnesses is arthritis. We're told that arthritis is a condition of age and nutrition, or it is congenital. Arthritis can be very painful and create extreme limitations in our mobility. Studies prove that almost every human being after a certain age has arthritis. However, some are severely limited by it while others show no limitations. What does that say? In essence, those being controlled by their fear, anxiety, hate, and anger, and who have not extended forgiveness to others or, more importantly, themselves, have created a powerful poison in their individual cells.

Too often, people contrive excuses for why they refuse to forgive. They find one argument after another to justify their individual stubbornness so they can remain in the prison they have created by not forgiving. All we need to do is to commit ourselves to forgive all those who have created disharmony in our lives in any way, shape, form, or matter in order to move forward in a positive way. There are cords that attach us to situations that have created the anger, frustration, pain, insecurity, doubt, fear, lack of self-worth, lack of self-esteem, and lack of pride between us and the situation, person, place, or thing. These cords create a circle of energy that keeps revolving, bringing forth feelings of discomfort, disharmony, and incompleteness. All those conditions that create the need for forgiveness put us in a circle of repetition, with all the negative energies resurfacing over and over again until active forgiveness is finally completed with unconditional love. The act of forgiveness breaks the cords to all those situations, persons, places, or things that created the need for forgiveness. Breaking the cords allows us to move about more freely and to heal. The best way to achieve this is through loving forgiveness. How can you truly love if you don't forgive and love yourself?

Step three involves a two-part process. The first is to write yourself a letter, using white paper with blue ink. Write down cause and origin of your frustration, anger, and pain. Next, write down the situation or circumstances that occurred at that time it appeared in your life. Then enumerate it in writing the negative effects it had upon your life. Ask yourself, "What am I to learn from this situation?" Once again, be sure to write it down. This is the next important step to take. Write down that you now forgive yourself; ask to have all cords attached to that situation as well as all cords attached to you be released. In private, look into a mirror. Then say three times, "I bless and release (name the situation or person) with love." Here is an example of how it should be done: "I (your name) release (name the person or situation) with love at all levels." Repeat three times. Then proceed to say, "I forgive (name of the person situation) with love at all levels." Repeat this process several times a day until you feel a shift of energy. When that occurs, the situation will be over and done with.

Forgiveness and compassionate understanding are the best way to achieve healing and self-love; love cannot be achieved without forgiveness and compassionate understanding, and forgiveness and compassionate understanding cannot be achieved without love.

"The supreme act of courage is that of forgiving ourselves. That which I was not but could have been. That which I would have done but did not do. Can I find the fortitude to remember in truth, to understand, to submit, to forgive and to be free to move on in time?"

— Martin Luther King, Jr.

EXERCISE

It is important that you write an explanation for each one of these questions.

Write down the most painful events in your past that made you angry.

_____

_____

_____

_____

_____

_____

_____

Observe where you feel each painful memory in your body and write it down.

_____

_____

_____

_____

_____

_____

_____

Answer the following questions for each memory separately. (Use a sheet of paper if you need more space.)

Why are you holding onto this emotion and pain?

_____

_____

_____

_____

_____

_____

_____

What positive emotion or feeling has it created in your life?

_____

_____

_____

_____

_____

_____

Why are you still hanging onto it?

_____

_____

_____

_____

_____

_____

_____

Are you ready to let go? If not, what will hanging onto it accomplish?

_____

_____

_____

_____

_____

_____

_____

When you are ready, release it with love, forgiving those you feel have hurt you and also forgiving yourself.

What does this energy of forgiveness feel like in your body?

_____

_____

_____

_____

_____

_____

_____

If you do not feel it, repeat this process until it is accomplished.

SUMMARY

Now that you have read this chapter, you have some very important decisions to make. Do you desire to let go of the past so you can enjoy an unlimited future? Are you willing to let go, forgive, and move forward for your own physical, mental, and emotional welfare? Are you ready to employ the techniques needed to release, heal, and become whole once again? It would behoove you to review the aforementioned techniques so you can become your authentic self.

"Forgiveness does not mean that we suppress anger; forgiveness means that we have asked for a miracle: the ability to see through mistakes that someone has made to the truth that lies in all our hearts. Forgiveness is not always easy. At times it feels more painful than the wound we suffered, to forgive the one that inflicted it. And yet, there is no peace without forgiveness. Attack thoughts towards others are attack thoughts towards ourselves. The first step in forgiveness is the willingness to forgive."

— Marianne Williamson

PART II

DISCOVERING YOUR PLACE IN THE UNIVERSE

Introduction to Discovering Your Place in the Universe

"The struggle ends when the gratitude begins."

— **Neale Donald Walsch**

Now that you understand the laws of the universe and how they operate, it's time for you to learn more about the other beings you share this universe with. In the chapters that follow, I will discuss your purpose in this world, and how you are not alone at all. Instead, you are partnering with numerous other beings who are helping you to fulfill your missions and goals on this planet. Some of those beings are your fellow humans; others are angels and other entities overseeing you and the planet to help you fulfill your purpose. Once you have a better understanding of them, you'll feel more confident in your ability to achieve your mission and goals.

In the wisdom and plan of God, the True Source, a goal was created to support our incarnation and what we have chosen to learn to accomplish in each and every life. Realize that you are being honored for choosing to learn and grow while simultaneously accomplishing your heavenly mission and goal on both the human and spiritual planes. As you read further, you will know and understand that you are never alone and all the assistance and tools you will need to accomplish your mission are being supplied to you. God, the True Source, as well as you yourself, knew this would be a Herculean job. That job might be best explained by comparing yourself to an architect. You are designing a home, your home. As you lay out the design, you have assistance from a whole army of carpenters, plumbers, electricians, roofers, etc. All of you are working as a team with the same common goal. This is what your incarnation looks like.

I congratulate you for taking the time to read this book and understand truly how special you are and the purpose of your incarnation.

Always know, without a doubt, that you are never alone or abandoned!

CHAPTER 13

THE GREAT GATHERING

"Be the change that you wish to see in the world."

— **Gandhi**

Take a minute to reflect on the words of Gandhi above because as you read the succeeding paragraphs, you will realize the importance of what is being requested of you.

I believe it is important for everyone to understand why we have guides, master guides, soulmates, twin souls, guardian angels, personal angels, and an entire hierarchy of angels. In God, the True Source's infinite wisdom, it was known that as our souls incarnated into different realms, vibrations, levels, and planets, a strong possibility existed that each one of us or a group of us would get lost in the energy, frequency, and vibration of that place. That is because the energy of some of these realms and planets was so dense that it could cause doubt, fear, and other emotional problems. In essence, the energy would cause us to forget who we are, why we are here, and our purpose. For that reason, we have spiritual partners to assist us.

I will discuss spiritual partnering in detail in the next chapter, but first, I want to make it clear that we all have a mission and goal on the human and spiritual planes. Plus, karma and karmic debts have to be answered for, whether the karma is positive or something that needs to be learned; either way, it helps you with your growth. You may be a newbie, so this is only your first lifetime, or you may have lost your way in previous lifetimes. Either way, human existence can create much confusion and feelings of being overwhelmed and lost. Therefore, each one of us is given the opportunity, if lost, to work our way back to connect with God, the True Source. God, the True Source, never ever gives up on us but always welcomes us back with open arms, unconditional love, and joy. That does not give us license to do negative things; however, it does give us the opportunity to heal any karma and begin again the journey of aligning ourselves with love, joy, harmony, peace, and the grace of God, the True Source. It is amazing how much depth and unconditional love, compassion, and understanding God, the True Source, has for you.

We are living during the time of the Great Gathering of Souls to bring about positive, loving, and heartfelt changes on the human plane, inner (spiritual) plane, and in your form (body). As I look about this planet, I see all kinds of pain, frustration, anger, futility, poverty, hopelessness, death, and disparity. There is very little love on our planet. It seems to be all about power, control, and greed. Some of you have gotten lost and have been caught up in the energy of confusion, anger, and frustration on this planet. Yet here we are, with a great gathering to bring about massive changes at all levels. You, the reader of this book, are part of the great gathering, and you are now charged with making great changes to create a huge difference. You see, this change is part of your mission and goal.

I have written this book because it is time to change humanity's consciousness so we can reconnect in a very powerful, direct way with God, the True Source. It is part of my mission and goal to help you realize and reconnect with God, the True Source, not only to bring love, joy, and healing to this planet and all around you, but also to remember your origins. In this way, you can make massive changes not only in your life, but in the lives of all whom you love and care about, including but not limited to your family. At the same time, you have the power and ability to save this planet and humankind. While this may seem a daunting task, it is best to remember that each one of us is an aspect of God, the True Source. Nothing, nothing is impossible. That gives us a true "heads up," plus invaluable tools and ability for the challenges forthcoming.

Be assured that we are winning and will win this battle, and it will be easier when we feel and know our reconnection to God, the True Source. This is where God, the True Source's Rule of Right Action and Correct Exchange comes into play. Throughout your many lifetimes, and even now, you have requested God, the True Source's assistance at all levels in your many lives. Now, God, the True Source, is asking you to work in concert following that part of the Rule of Right Action and Correct Exchange. Once we make our connection with God, the True Source, we are individually and jointly able to participate in correct exchange by changing and healing this planet and its inhabitants. What an honor and joy for you to take part in this!

Some of you may be wondering how this healing will be accomplished! I am not sure of the intricate details, but just the big picture that shows each one of us, you and I, as successful. We are the force that, through our reconnection to God, the True Source, will make the monumental changes needed. The gathering has begun and now great positive changes are taking place. It is a joy for me to realize that as you are reading this book, you are allowing yourself to be part of this great change. How wonderful to be aware of the great part you are making in this corner of the universe on this beautiful planet. Congratulations!

EXERCISE

Begin the Dream Heaven mantra.

In your meditation, set the intention to know what changes you need to make. When revealed to you, write down what those changes are.

_____

_____

_____

After you have ascertained what they are, ask for assistance in obtaining the changes with love, joy, grace, harmony, and ease. Then, write down what you are going to do each day to make the necessary changes in your life.

_____

_____

_____

SUMMARY

This book is all about you discovering who you are and what is your sacred path. You now have begun a new journey to awaken from your deep slumber into a life you have always dreamt of. It is important to remember that your life is like a blank canvas and you are the artist. You can draw, paint, or create a new life from this point forward. Your life now becomes filled with unlimited choices, all leading in one direction—to a renewed and invigorated you, and ultimately, to the healing of the planet. Welcome to the great gathering!

CHAPTER 14

SPIRITUAL PARTNERING

*"To believe in the things you can see and touch is no belief at all, but
to believe in the unseen is both a triumph and a blessing."*

— Bob Proctor

As I explained in the last chapter, when we left the bosom of
God, the True Source, and incarnated into human form, we lowered
our vibrations. As a result, we have largely forgotten our spiritual
origins so we need assistance from beings such as guides and angels
to help us stay on the right path. In this chapter, we will explore the
various ways that other entities partner with us so we can fulfill our
missions and goals on this earth.

TWIN SOULS

As we incarnated into different forms, we formed partnerships,
one of which is called "twin souls." Twin souls are spiritual beings,
entities, who have agreed to take on the same life path we do in

order to create all that exists in the universe through enlightenment and completing our missions and goals so we can achieve spiritual growth in our chosen paths.

Our twin souls may be of the opposite or same sex. Often, they incarnate at the same time, although one may incarnate while the other works in another vibration known as the spiritual or inner plane. This is done so they have a multidimensional approach for achieving their missions and goals. It is very rare that you will meet your twin soul in the human plane. However, I have been blessed to meet the person whom I believe is my twin soul. In this lifetime, my twin soul is female. What is so uncanny is that whatever occurs to her first occurs to me later or vice versa. One day, she called me and during our conversation she mentioned that her nails were breaking; I laughed because so were mine. Another time, she said she had just bought some hummus, and that same day, I had bought the same thing. We have had several experiences beyond coincidence that have made us both come to the conclusion that we are twin souls. More importantly, we are on the same path to help souls of this planet and elsewhere to reconnect with God, the True Source. Our spiritual backgrounds are different, but we have the same goals and reach similar conclusions. What is joyous about our relationship is that we share with each other the techniques we use to achieve our spiritual growth and enlightenment, and we are always in tune with one another. Our relationship is special because we support each other unconditionally and are always spiritually loving toward all and one another. What a unique blessing for both of us.

By connecting with your twin soul, you will find that you are never alone, you are fully supported, and you will always be reminded of your connection to God, the True Source. Your twin soul will teach you that all things are possible through telepathic messages, dreams, and whatever vehicle he or she can use to convey the message to you. It could be in the form of a song or an article you suddenly read or a message someone gives you or a dream. The important thing is that you do not have to worry whether messages are coming from your twin soul or not. The messages will be made very evident in a way that you cannot misunderstand. It's more like a light bulb going off throughout your body, calling your attention to the message. While the feeling is hard to explain, once you have felt it—and you will—you will be able to discern what is your ego or your imagination and what is reality. It is always joyous to know that we are not alone and that we are working in tandem with our twin soul.

EXERCISE

While performing the Dream Heaven mantra, ask for clarity regarding the information listed below. Keep repeating until you have success.

Ask to sense and feel your twin soul. Write down what you are feeling.

What are you feeling?

_____

_____

_____

What are you telepathically hearing and sensing?

_____

_____

_____

SOULMATES

By this point, you are wondering what is a soulmate. Simply answered, when we left to take on a physical form, we divided ourselves in half or more to accomplish our goals and missions more easily and rapidly. Therefore, your soulmate is your opposite half. If you are male in this incarnation, then your soulmate would be female or vice versa. Your personalities may complement one another, but they are different in various aspects, for remember, your soulmate is your opposite. This begs the question: What if you are gay or bisexual? The answer is that, in spiritual form, we all are androgynous. Therefore, whatever energy or guidance is needed for you, your twin soul, guides, master guides, and guardian angels will take on at vibration that can best help and serve you. This also applies to all souls who have incarnated in embodiment no matter what sex they have chosen or their sexuality. It is key to remember that all of us possess the energy, vibrations, and frequency of everything that has ever been created. Henceforth, the expression "We are all one."

If you are seeking your soulmate in this life, know that if you find your soulmate, the relationship can be very loving, caring, and beautiful, but it can also be extremely challenging for both of you if you are not willing to embrace God, the True Source's love and your mutual mission and goal in life. That said, it is rare that soulmates will both incarnate at the same time. Furthermore, when they do incarnate at the same time, it does not necessarily mean they will marry one another since they may incarnate in different places on this planet and never meet in their shared lifetime. Either way, both are working on the spiritual and human planes to accomplish similar goals. If your soulmate does not incarnate simultaneously with you, he or she can still be working with you on the human plane.

He or she may also be working at different levels on the spiritual plane or in any universe with similar goals and missions.

Most people expect their soulmates to be in perfect alignment with them; while this may happen, usually soulmates' personalities are opposite. Marrying your soulmate sounds very romantic, but it can be very challenging or very rewarding, depending upon your spiritual alignment and human ego. In reality, if you are shy, your soulmate will be verbose; if you are mild-mannered or easy-going, he or she may be hot-tempered and aggressive. However, as I said, it is still possible to have harmony with your soulmate if you are enlightened enough and realize this.

Whether you meet and marry your soulmate in this lifetime or not, it is exciting to know you have a teammate called your soulmate working with you to help you in all your endeavors.

EXERCISE

Start with the Dream Heaven mantra. Remember to inhale "dream" and exhale "heaven" 108 times.

Before you begin your mantra, place the intention that you desire to meet your soulmate on the spiritual plane. Whether your soulmate has incarnated or not, it makes no difference because you can meet them more easily on the spiritual plane.

Ask to feel your soulmate's energy and record below what you are feeling.

What are you feeling emotionally?

_____

_____

_____

What are you telepathically hearing in your mind and/or sensing?

_____

_____

_____

Ask for clarity to receive these thoughts in your mind and body. Keep repeating the mantra until you have success.

SPIRITUAL SPOUSES

If you're not already confused, there is also what is known as a spiritual spouse. Your spiritual spouse is just that! It is either your wife or your husband, depending upon your sex in this incarnation. The reason your spouse is of the opposite sex is he or she brings in the energy frequency and vibrations needed for you to do your human and spiritual work. If you are LGBT, then your spiritual spouse will bring forth the energy you need to balance your own. Once again, as I mentioned previously, we are all androgynous. Your spiritual spouse was created by your design with the assistance of God, the True Source. It was felt that the God-force energy of love needed to be experienced on planes of lower vibrations (dimensions) so that those who left the creator's bosom would be reminded of God, the True Sources' unconditional love energy and its origin. In essence, your spiritual spouse is there to help you remember the energy in case you get lost or forget. Each spiritual spouse's job is to remind the other of love and to work in tandem with the other to assist in his or her assigned missions and goals or those he or she has chosen to complete. Your spiritual spouse is unconditionally loving, allowing, and nonjudgmental. He or she is always with you to assist you in all things that you do as long as it is right action and correct exchange. This means that your spiritual spouse is always there to assist you in all your endeavors when you request his or her help. It also ensures that both of you will work in tandem, assisting one another and God, the True Source.

When I began to understand about spiritual spouses, I was over-joyed and wanted to meet mine. Because I am a heterosexual male, the energy of my spiritual spouse would be female, but it is best to remember that our essence of beingness is actually androgynous.

To find your spiritual spouse, you need to begin the process of meditation, asking to link up first on an energetic level, then on a vibrational frequency level, and then on the human emotional level. Once you achieve this, you will be amazed by your initial en-counter and realize that your spiritual spouse has always been with you since the very beginning of your creation and is always with you. Your spiritual spouse is always willing to assist you and enable you to achieve your missions and goals, including, but not limited to, bringing love, joy, happiness, perfect health, and prosperity, and even bringing in your made-in-heaven miracle mate. I know now you're wondering, *What is a made-in-heaven miracle mate?* Hang in there. I'll discuss it next. But for now, I feel it is important that you begin the process of linking up and aligning yourself with your spiritual spouse.

I am always amazed by the love and caring that God, the True Source, has for us by creating all these beautiful entities and souls to remind us of our connection and our missions and goals. Your true spiritual spouse is truly incredible; he or she will always be there to remind you of your connections.

EXERCISE

Once again, as before, begin your Dream Heaven meditation with your two bowls and 108 items. Set your intention to feel the energy and love of your spiritual spouse. Then ask yourself the following questions and write down your responses.

Ask to feel the unconditional love of your spiritual spouse. What does it feel like?

_____

_____

_____

_____

_____

_____

What are you sensing?

_____

_____

_____

_____

_____

What are you telepathically hearing?

_____

_____

_____

_____

_____

What are you seeing in your third eye?

_____

_____

_____

_____

_____

_____

Ask whether there is a message for you and that you can hear it clearly in your thoughts.

_____

_____

_____

_____

_____

_____

As always, continue this exercise until you have achieved your desired goal. Patience is most important as well as stick-to-itiveness.

MADE-IN-HEAVEN MIRACLE MATE

By now, I guess I have kept you in suspense long enough. What is your made-in-heaven miracle mate? Before you incarnated, you understood that there were certain relationships that you had to bring to closure. Some were on a family basis, e.g., mothers, fathers, siblings, children, and relatives. Also, there are business relationships, friendships, and relationships with lovers and spouses that were either to be brought to closure or to last a lifetime. But I would like to address at this time that sometimes there are love relationships that were meant to be temporary for one reason or another. Those who have brought to closure a spousal relationship and are seeking another long-term relationship have the possibility of bringing forth their made-in-heaven miracle mate. This can also be requested as your very first relationship in this incarnation. Your made-in-heaven miracle mate is best described as your true friend, someone who is unconditionally loving, nonjudgmental, supportive, and the love of your life. Someone who brings about a loving physical, mental, emotional, and spiritual relationship. This love is the kind written about in novels and depicted in movies. Some of you who are reading this book are now wondering how you can bring forth your made-in-heaven miracle mate. First of all, I caution you only to do this if you are single. Perhaps you already are with your made-in-heaven miracle mate.

To prepare for this, repeat the exercise of Dream Heaven. The next step is to ask God, the True Source, to bring forth your made-in-heaven miracle mate in such a way that there is no doubt who he or she is. Repeat this request for nine days in a row either in the morning or just before you go to sleep. Once this has been completed, you may relax, knowing at the perfect time that he or she will show up!

I am always amazed by the love and caring that God, the True Source, has for us by creating all these beautiful entities and souls to remind us of our connection and missions and goals. Your true spiritual spouse is truly incredible; he or she will always be there to remind you of your connections.

EXERCISE

Once again, as before, begin your Dream Heaven meditation with your two bowls and 108 items. Set your intention to feel the energy and love of your made-in-heaven miracle mate. Then ask yourself the following questions and write down your responses.

Ask to feel the unconditional love of your made-in-heaven miracle mate. What does it feel like?

_____

_____

_____

_____

_____

_____

What are you sensing?

_____

_____

_____

_____

_____

_____

What are you telepathically hearing?

_____

_____

_____

_____

_____

_____

What are you seeing in your third eye?

_____

_____

_____

_____

_____

_____

Ask whether there is a message for you and that you can hear it clearly in your thoughts.

_____

_____

_____

_____

_____

_____

As always, continue this exercise until you have achieved your desired goal. Patience is most important as well as stick-to-itiveness.

GUARDIAN ANGELS

As time went by and we began to incarnate, we began to create a vehicle, known as a body, to house our frequencies, vibrations, and energies. At this point, we began to fulfill our missions and goals, which could include, but are not limited to, creating new vibrations, frequencies, levels of spirituality, planets, animals, fish, rocks, plant life, and other forms and items needed to sustain our new housing called bodies. Simultaneously, some souls sought to be like and were jealous of God, the True Source. Sound familiar? A similar version of this story is told in the Bible about angels and fallen angels. These souls or entities sought to influence and control other souls who came later to achieve their missions and goals. These negative entities became quite persuasive and convinced some souls that had incarnated in different forms to create chaos in multiple ways. We see some of this now throughout this planet.

Long, long ago, it was requested by previous souls that had incarnated and were challenged by the negative jealous souls that those souls that had not yet incarnated and were still in the bosom of God, the True Source, would assist them. Consequently, it was determined that each soul that left the bosom of God, the True Source, would have a "backup" called a guardian angel. The name itself describes a guardian angel's duties. In the very beginning, guardian angels protected all souls that had incarnated. Their job was to be in constant contact with incarnated souls to protect them from and alert them to any dangers.

In general, most souls only have one guardian angel, but some may have more depending upon their missions and goals on the human and spiritual planes. While the average is one guardian angel, some have two or three or more. The more copious your missions and goals, the more guardian angels you have to assist you.

As I explained earlier, some incarnated souls may forget their missions and goals and become lost. In these cases, it is the job of your guardian angels to protect you on the physical, mental, spiritual, and emotional planes. Guardian angels make sure we do not put ourselves in harm's way while aiding us in fulfilling our missions and goals.

Many wonderful stories have been told about guardian angels, but I would like to share my own personal stories. Many years ago, I lived in Tallman, New York, which is near Spring Valley, New York, and about fifty miles from New York City. I had an office in New York City where I was involved in marketing and sales. One day, I locked my keys in my car and had to take a train back to Tallman, New York, to get my other set of keys. You can't leave your car overnight on the mean streets of New York City or it will be completely stripped the next morning, so my wife, friend, and I drove back to New York City so I could pick up my car. After unlocking my car, I began the long journey home.

Returning to Tallman required crossing the Tappan Zee Bridge, a huge multi-mile bridge that crosses the Hudson River and is several hundred feet tall. It was summer, it had just rained, and the temperature was approximately 90°. Since it had not rained for a long time, the recent rain had caused a fine layer of oil and grease from the cars to become a slick puddle on the bridge. All of a sudden, my car began to swerve. I began to turn the wheels in the opposite direction to try to stop the car from swerving. However, it only got worse. I tried the next best thing, which was to step on the accelerator, believing that the wheels would begin to spin and correct the swerving. All this did was increase my speed and cause me to spin in concentric circles. As my car neared a guardrail, I feared my car would crash through the guardrail and fall into the water, some several hundred feet below. I could only hope that I would survive.

I began silently praying to God, the True Source, my guardian angel, and the other angels to protect me. At the same time, I heard the thought, *Hit the brakes hard and you will be okay.* Desperate and fearful, that is exactly what I did. All of a sudden, my car stopped about eight inches before the guardrail. As I looked down the lane of opposing traffic, which I was now in, I saw an eighteen-wheeler barreling down on me. Fortunately, I had time to turn the car around in the opposite direction and make it off the bridge. At this point, I pulled over to the side, my heart pounding, and gave thanks to God, the True Source, my guardian angel, and all the angels for protecting me. It was a very harrowing experience, but at the same time, I felt blessed, protected, and lucky to be loved by my guardian angel and the other angels.

Another time, I was in college in Albany, New York. One night, it had just snowed, and I was driving down a steep hill, knowing it would be slippery, so I was not going more than three or four miles per hour. Regardless, my car began to lose traction. Soon, it was spinning in circles as I was going down the hill for almost 300 feet and toward the intersection at the bottom. The experience was quite scary, and I did everything I believe you are supposed to do in this situation, including pumping the brakes. Once again, I called upon God, the True Source, my guardian angel, and the other angels to protect me. When I arrived at the bottom of the hill, my car stopped spinning in the intersection, although turned in the opposite direction it should be. Miraculously, there was a break in the traffic some 300 feet in each direction which allowed me to turn my car around to exit a dangerous, life-threatening situation.

Another story concerns my sister. Since she is four years older than I, she was quite jealous when I was born because she was no longer getting all the attention. Years later, she asked me whether I still loved her. Of course, I replied, "Yes." She then told me about four incidents I had survived as a small child. The first time, I was approximately a year old and she was five. She took a pillow and put it over my head to try to suffocate me. I was probably crying, and she did not realize the severity of what she was doing. Fortunately, my mother came in just in time to prevent any serious damage. The second time, I was two years old and in a baby carriage. Our apartment complex had a swimming pool, and my sister pushed the baby carriage into the pool. Once again, my mother rescued me. The third time, I was three years old. My sister decided to take me for a ride in the wagon and ended up pushing the wagon down a steep hill. Once again, I miraculously survived the situation without a scratch. The fourth and last time, I was five and she was nine. I was riding my tricycle when my sister pushed me into traffic. Once again, I was protected by my guardian angel and other angels so no harm came to me. Today, my sister and I have a very close and loving relationship. After she reminded me of these incidents, I totally and completely forgave her. I'm sure you can remember times when you, too, were protected by both your guardian angel and other angels.

EXERCISE

Start with the Dream Heaven exercise. Begin your meditation as before, and set your intention to meet, see, and feel your guardian angel.

Ask to sense the energy of your guardian angel and record your feelings.

_____

_____

_____

Ask to feel your guardian angel around you. What does it feel like?

_____

_____

_____

Ask to see your guardian angel when the time is appropriate for you. What answer do you feel?

_____

_____

_____

Ask whether your guardian angel has a message for you and to receive it in your thoughts with great clarity. Write it down.

_____

_____

_____

Never give up on this exercise until you achieve your desired results. Your guardian angels are here to protect you, and if you will listen and pay attention, you will realize how safe and protected you are.

GUIDES AND MASTER GUIDES

Through the wisdom of God, the True Source, and upon each soul's request, it was decided before we incarnated that we would have additional assistance to help keep us on our life paths to achieve our missions and goals on the human and spiritual planes. Before we incarnate, we choose one or more missions and goals we desire to accomplish in any given lifetime. We look at various scenarios, situations, and families that will assist us in completing our missions and goals. Once we have chosen those scenarios, situations, and families, we then ask for specific guides and master guides to assist us in our incarnation endeavors. Guides are usually entities (souls) who have worked their way up the ladder (hierarchy) to become first guides and eventually master guides, etc. A master guide's job is to oversee the neophyte guides and our souls. They have the same common task, which is to assist us in achieving our mission and goal. They too, are also working up the ladder of hierarchy to become angels, etc.

Each one of us has, at one time or another, run into figurative brick walls or had challenges in trying to accomplish something that would not work out, no matter how hard we tried. You likely tried different courses in school, different colleges or degree programs, different jobs, or even different relationships that did not work out or may have even been disasters. These situations may have felt like being a quarterback on a football team with no players while still trying to reach the goal line to score points. When these situations arise, it's because you are not listening to that little voice from your guides or master guides that is telling you this is not what you had planned to accomplish in this lifetime. That is because you became lost and seduced by different goals and situations due to outside influences from families, relationships, or fears. That little voice, or perhaps it's a gut feeling, is telling you that you are off course. All you need to do is to ask for your guides and master guides to direct you and just let it occur. That sounds too simplistic, doesn't it? And, yes, it is simple and easy, if you can just get out of our own way and either enlist or ask for your guides and master guides to open the proper doors and direct you on the correct path to fulfill your goals and missions and to complete your karma.

Let me tell you a story about a time when my guides helped me. At the time, I was in the nursing home business in a Boston suburb. I was feeling extreme stress on this particular day from dealing with the patients, nurses, hospitals, etc. By about 4:30 or 5:00 p.m., the stress had become so overwhelming that I began to feel a bulge on the right side of my temple. At first, I ignored it, but soon, it became more pronounced and uncomfortable. I feared I was going to have a cerebral hemorrhage. My assistant, who was very spiritual, saw what was happening. She asked me to sit in my recliner while she performed reiki—a form of energy healing—on me. I agreed, so she placed her hands along the sides of my temple. As she worked, I called upon my guides, master guides, and the healing angels to heal me in whatever way possible.

All of a sudden, she told me she felt an energy coming into her hands and she locked her hands onto my head. At the same time, she also said she felt my mother, whom she had never met or known and who was deceased, enter into her body to work with my guides, master guides, and the angels to assist in healing me. I was very impatient, even looking at my watch. After a few minutes, however, I began to space out and lose track of time. The only thing I could feel were her hands locked onto the sides of my head. After some time, I became aware again and realized I was now back in my body. I could also feel the bulging decreasing and eventually disappearing. She held onto my temples for a few more minutes. Then I looked at the time and could not believe that more than forty-five minutes had passed with her hands locked onto my head. I felt drained, re-laxed, and ready to sleep. My guides, master guides, and angels had worked in concert, this time with my mother, to assist in healing and protecting me, for which I am eternally grateful.

Guides and master guides are always with us to assist us in our mission goals while at the same time helping each one of us to grow and remember our connection with God, the True Source. Not only do our guides and master guides keep us on the paths we have chosen to experience, but they also work in tandem with our guardian angels and other spiritual beings to assist us. Many people have asked me how many guides and master guides each soul brings with it to assist it in its reincarnation. The number can be as little as one or many more. It all depends upon our missions and goals and our karma.

It is a joy to know that we are never alone and that we have assistants like our guides, master guides, and guardian angel(s) always there to work and protect us on both the spiritual and human planes.

EXERCISE

Start with the Dream Heaven meditation. Set your intention to meet your guides and master guides.

Ask to feel the energy of your guides and master guides.

Ask to see your guides and master guides when the time is appropriate.

Ask them to give you a message with clarity in your thoughts. Write it down.

_____

_____

_____

_____

_____

_____

Do not give up; keep repeating this exercise until you have succeeded.

Guides and master guides are here to keep you on track with your missions and goals. Listen to your thoughts and inner guidance rather than fight with your ego in order to accomplish what you came here to do.

ANGELS, ARCHANGELS, AND THE HIGHER ORDER OF ANGELS

To begin this discussion of angels, I would like to share a story about how angels obtain their wings. The early fifteenth century artists, sculptors, and painters were able to use their third eye to visualize in their mind what they desired to paint or sculpture. Because their third eye was so finely honed for their particular creativity, they were able to see translucent beings move around the room where they were creating their art. These beings seemed to move from one point to another in the room very quickly. It appeared as if they seemed to fly around the artists and throughout the room. The artists were puzzled as to how these beings could go from point A to B so quickly. Since they had observed how birds move through the air using their wings, they came to the conclusion that these beings must also have wings. This bit of mythology grew until it became the accepted norm. The angels decided that since most humans believed they had wings, they would appear to us in that way. It is a beautiful story, and in my mind, it makes total sense.

I would like to use a metaphor to take you on a mental journey with me. For a moment, pretend you are Henry Ford. You decide you're going to make some kind of vehicle that will go from point A to point B, and you'll call it an automobile. You then obtain a building and hire some workers. Since it is a new venture, your workers will be receiving what will be called on-the-job training. They will all work together as a team to create the perfect vehicle. As you begin to make the vehicle and you become more and more successful, you realize you not only need to keep improving the vehicle, but you need to hire more employees. As you hire more employees, you realize you need several managers, supervisors, trainers, and other leaders to oversee the employees. In fact, you become so successful that you have to open plants all over the planet and elsewhere, hiring more and more people and having more and more supervisors and managers. Because you are using so many products—tires, spark plugs, etc.—you need to form more companies or hire other companies to supply your needs. Your manufacturing plants begin to expand and expand, seemingly without limit.

I'm using this simple analogy for you to understand how the universe works. The universe's evolution is much more complex than my analogy, but there is a definite order to it, and it keeps expanding.

At first, only a few of us incarnated, but later, more and more of us came forward. Consequently, there needed to be structure, form, and a hierarchy to oversee what we were creating and to keep harmony and balance. In essence, that is what angels do.

Through your incarnations, you attract assistance from angels to help you with your missions and goals. I've met souls who have angels assisting them in small numbers and others who have in excess of one million angels assisting them. The greater the number of angels the soul has with him or her, the greater that person's missions and goals. Having one angel can accomplish miracles beyond one's imagination. Having more means you have taken on a great task and need all of them to assist you. It is wonderful to know that you are not alone; no matter how difficult your life may be on the human plane, you always have backup. What is truly amazing and awe-inspiring is how God, the True Source, has designed everything to be in harmony and balance, including all humans, the universe, and all things that exist.

The archangels' task is to maintain harmony and balance for each planet, making sure the negativity does not destroy it. The archangels sometimes work with individual souls because they have common goals. Nevertheless, these archangels are always unconditionally loving, allowing, and nonjudgmental, and if we ask, they will assist us. In addition, the archangels work with the energies of their respective planets and other parts of the universe to achieve and create harmony and balance. You might ask, "Where are the archangels right now?" since we have such huge discordant energy with the souls on this planet at this time. As I have said before, we have free will and free choice. There are negative influences out there bent on creating chaos, fear, disillusionment, and confusion; however, I assure you a master plan exists to all things, and it is being worked out on this planet and in this corner of the universe. The end result will be, at first, individual enlightenment and reconnection to God, the True Source, and later on, a positive change of consciousness will occur that will help us all. It will assist us to reconnect with love and oneness to God, the True Source. The same applies to other higher orders of angels, e.g., the Elohim. Their job is to keep order and balance in the universe with all that has been created and exists and that will exist in the future.

EXERCISE

Start with the Dream Heaven exercise. Ask the following questions as you meditate. After the exercise, write down your feelings, emotions, and what you perceive or feel.

Ask to sense the archangels and higher orders of angels' energies.

_____

_____

_____

_____

Ask to feel the angels' presence.

_____

_____

_____

_____

Ask to see the angels.

_____

_____

_____

_____

Ask the angels for a clear message in your mind.

_____

_____

_____

_____

Do not become discouraged if you do not succeed in receiving responses at first. Keep repeating this exercise. You will achieve your goal.

Isn't it wonderful to know that you are never alone but fully connected to God, the True Source, and in God, the True Source's wisdom, you are surrounded by heavenly beings that protect you, love you, assist you, and help you grow. No greater love can be bestowed upon you to achieve your goals than what has already been given to you.

"If you wish to reach the highest, begin at the lowest."

— Publilius Syrus

MEETING GOD, THE TRUE SOURCE

I would like to share with you at this time some beautiful information that was presented to me by God, the True Source. In my youth, I began to search for more knowledge and enlightenment. The one question that kept coming up over and over again in my thoughts was: What purpose does religion have in our lives? I was told that the purpose of all religions was to set up some type of moral code to create order and, in some religions, subservience. Some religions' rules and regulations were created by humankind to control others; some were created by negative entities, and some by those whose missions and goals were from God, the True Source. We need only to look at the Ten Commandments to find an example of a moral code. Some of its rules include: Thou shall not kill; Honor thy mother and father; and Thou shall not bear false witness. Other religions influenced by mankind created laws that would punish anyone who did not follow that specific religion; punishments ranged from telling people they would burn in hell to actually burning people at the stake and more.

God, the True Source, pointed out to me that others like myself have sought to go beyond some, but not all, of religion's limitations.

As I question and seek more knowledge, more understanding comes to me. As I travel and meet many spiritual souls, I find that some are growing while others become stuck because of their religious or spiritual beliefs. I do not wish to criticize them, but you always need to continue to grow and search. My evolution started with guides, and later on master guides, angels, archangels, and other higher orders of angels until I was finally able to connect with God, the True Source.

I would now like to share how I connected with God, the True Source. In my quest for enlightenment, as I worked my way toward that goal, I eventually made a connection with God, the True Source. In our initial meeting, I asked this being whether it was God. The Divine told me it was not in the way that humans perceive God to be. When I asked why, the True Source told me that God, the True Source, does not cause illness; souls to be killed; divorces; loss of prosperity and abundance; physical, mental, and emotional pain; loss of jobs; wars, etc. God, the True Source, said, "I do not even want your money." I began to understand why God, the True Source, did not like the word God—because the word has been abused and bastardized by despots like Napoleon and Hitler. I understood that a division between people has occurred as a result of this usage of the word God by such despots. Many people lose their faith in God when God's name is used to justify atrocities. Henceforth, I ceased to use the word God and instead used the term, the True Source. To provide clarity for my readers, however, I have used the term God, the True Source.

I then asked God, the True Source, what the real rules are. There are only three of them, and I will share them with you as they were related to me:

Everything that exists in the universe is an aspect of the God, the True Source. Therefore, anything I desire I have to ask for; I cannot expect it to be given to me. By asking for it, I will receive it.

I have to use right action and correct exchange when I request something. In essence, you cannot ask for something negative. Correct exchange means "pay it forward." You could receive God, the True Source's inner guidance to assist the Divine in a special project.

Everything occurs in the True Source's time, which is the perfect time requested by you.

As you can see, the rules are pretty simple and yet so powerful. God, the True Source, also pointed out to me that I was given free will so I could experience everything, even if it wasn't right action. The beautiful part of this, as told to me by God, the True Source, is that if I get off my path, I can ask permission to get back on it and there will be total forgiveness because God, the True Source, loves everything and everyone unconditionally, and there is never any judgment. How beautiful, how true, and how empowering. Just imagine for a moment if everyone on this planet followed the rule of right action and correct exchange—how much more pleasant, joyous, and loving this planet would be. Sometimes, the most complex things we desire are so simple. When I have shared these wonderful revelations with my friends and students, miracles of joy, happiness, prosperity, and love have come into their lives.

It is such a joy for me to be charged with sharing this information to help you reconnect to God, the True Source, so you can achieve a life beyond your wildest dreams or perhaps what you have always wished for. Know now that the doors are open for you to achieve it.

"When I let go of what I am, I become what I might be."

— Lao Tzu

My Spiritual Path

I would like to share my story of how I began my spiritual path in earnest. Many years ago, my dream was to become a very successful entrepreneur. I had owned several successful businesses and was now engaged in the nursing home business. This was my first venture into the nursing home business and I enjoyed it immensely, so much that I wanted to purchase more nursing homes. Each time a nursing home went up for sale, I consulted my financial team and lawyer to see whether I could buy it. At this time, I also learned from God, the True Source, a specific powerful affirmation. Simply put, I asked that if that nursing home was not the right business for me to purchase, that all the negotiations would fall apart immediately. However, when one after another fell apart, I forgot I had invoked that affirmation. After some frustration and anxiety, I realized why these negotiations fell apart, but my ego still wanted to know whether I had made a mistake.

I would like to share a story about one of the nursing homes I began negotiations to purchase. The state of Massachusetts' legal department for nursing homes confidentially told me that this particular nursing home would be tough to operate because the state's financial nursing home division would not give me enough money for Medicare patients so that I could operate this particular home properly. As time went by, I observed that all the nursing homes that had fallen apart in my negotiations had all gone bankrupt under the new owners. Needless to say, my faith became stronger and stronger in God, the True Source.

At one point in the mid-1980s, the Massachusetts Department of Nursing Homes' reimbursement division claimed it had a computer problem. It was only paying Medicare and Medicaid patients less than 50 percent of the money needed to take care of them. This situation made it difficult for nursing homes, including mine, to provide adequate care for the patients. I was told the situation was temporary; however, it lasted just over a year. What little financial reserves I had were quickly used up. I then asked God, the True Source, for assistance; soon after I learned that my suppliers had extended my credit; my banker even called me up to ask how he could help out, and they extended my credit farther by giving me a loan. I never did find out why the state had the so-called computer glitch, but I'm sure it was playing some kind of financial game because in those days, interest rates were as high as 18 percent. Once again, I was protected because I was able to get loans at a much lower interest rate. This is just another example of how God, the True Source, was looking out for me when I requested help. Similarly, know that whatever you ask for shall be taken care of and given to you.

Despite the help I received, initially I was under a great deal of stress from worrying about finances, my patients, and state inspections. Then I had an experience in which my guardian angels, other angels, and God, the True Source, protected me. A little while later, God, the True Source, came to me and gave me a choice of either becoming a multimillionaire or being very spiritual. The words "spiritual path" spewed forth from my lips. I thought, *Why did I say that? What a silly statement to make.* However, my whole life began to change thereafter, including my going through a divorce. I went back to college to obtain dual bachelor and master's degrees in Human Services and Gerontology. Later, I went on to get a doctorate. Then God, the True Source, through spirit, told me to move to the West Coast. I had family living in California, which was my interpretation of "West Coast." But I was not in love with the heat and the bareness of the topography there compared to that of New England. I was told that it didn't matter whether I move from Massachusetts to Michigan, then to South Carolina, then to Florida, and then back to Boston because, ultimately, I would move to the West Coast. Well, guess what? Today, I live near Seattle, Washington—the West Coast. I learned never to argue with God, the True Source.

Magic occurred on my way out to the West Coast. One of my goals was to visit Pottstown, Pennsylvania, where I was born. At that time, I had an Akita dog named Daysue, who was very spiritual and protective in his own right. I purchased a truck, packed up my few belongings, and set off for a grand adventure. I asked God, the True Source, to help me find a shortcut to Pottstown, Pennsylvania. Traveling through Connecticut, I drove into a truck stop and pulled alongside an eighteen-wheeler moving van with large lettering indicating it was from Pottstown, Pennsylvania. When I asked the driver the best way to get to Pottstown, he was most helpful. That synchronicity took place each and every moment throughout my whole trip. Daysue and I were protected, and we both an incredibly fun trip.

Something wonderful occurred for me during that trip. I was a typical "A" personality who will work and work and work. The gift I received from God, the True Source, was I became more relaxed, more at ease, and physically and emotionally healed. On the way out to Washington, I also crisscrossed the United States and met some very beautiful, wonderful, and helpful souls. I had the opportunity to see triple rainbows and other strange things in the sky, which I interpreted as positive signs. Because I had a dog and most motels back then would not allow dogs in their rooms, I camped out in various places across the country. This was truly a leap of faith for me because I did not know where I was going to live, where I was going to stay, or how I was going to make a living. As it was, I received a call from a friend of mine from Massachusetts who was moving to Chehalis, Washington, and he offered me a place to live. Wow! I could not believe that this was happening.

In retrospect, God, the True Source, truly works in wondrous ways. Shortly after arriving in Washington, I obtained a job as a professor of economics, marketing, and business communications at City University in Bellevue, Washington. I taught at Bellevue and its various satellites. I also received a part-time job at Griffin Community College teaching English and Psychology 101. I continued to be amazed by God, the True Source's unconditional love and abundance. Because I had multiple degrees in Human Services and Gerontology, someone had recommended me to US West Telephone Company. When I was interviewed by the company, I was asked whether I would use my expertise in gerontology to recommend caller ID to the state of Washington's legislators as a valuable tool for the elderly. I agreed, with the thought in mind that I would receive a job offer from US West Telephone Company. I proceeded to speak on behalf of US West Telephone Company, and after I spoke, the legislators immediately took a vote, which passed overwhelmingly in favor of providing caller ID. Many individual legislators came up to me to congratulate me on my excellent presentation. I thought this was wonderful and would lead to a job with US West Telephone Company. Much to my chagrin, the company took me out to lunch and then told me I was overqualified to work for them. I felt dismayed, but at the same time, happy that I was able to assist the elderly in obtaining what I considered an important tool.

One day, having nothing to do and at the same time feeling bored, I wandered into a metaphysical shop. I looked around and heard a message from God, the True Source. The message was "Welcome back! Time to start teaching." It was almost as if this event were prearranged between God, the True Source, and the metaphysical shop's owners. The owners asked whether I was an intuitive. When I replied, "Yes," they asked whether I would be interested in doing psychic readings on weekends. I agreed, and it worked out well since I was still teaching during the week at the colleges.

After a couple of months, people started asking me whether I would teach them how to do readings. My reply was an emphatic "No!" After being badgered by the metaphysical shop's owner and clientele, I finally acquiesced. I then talked to God, the True Source, explaining that if I were to teach, it was not because I desired to be a guru but merely because I wanted to help them awaken. In reply, God, the True Source, told me I did not need to read any books to teach. Instead, I would be taught by God, the True Source, using the True Source's "created resources." The created resources are the guides, master guides, angels, and archangels, which would work with me and guide me. I also learned that information from my past lives would come forth in my teaching.

Before I knew it, I was teaching four nights a week with approximately thirty-five students per class. I told them that this course was only three months long. After a few weeks, my students told me they were having dreams that I was going to be teaching them for three years. I laughed and said, "Nope. It is only for three months!" As you probably have guessed, the course extended out to three years. At that time, I told them "Congratulations" and "It's time for you to move on." I reiterated that I was there for them if they had any questions. I told them all that I loved them and wished them the very best. However, one group of them continued to badger me because they wanted to learn more. I resisted them for three years, but I finally gave in.

What is amazing to me is that God, the True Source, has continued to guide and direct me through all the years I have been teaching, which is now more than twenty-five. Even more amazing, I have only repeated teaching two or three of the classes over that time. I guess my message to all of you reading this book is that you will never stop growing and learning unless you put the brakes on; in other words, your ability to learn is unlimited because you're loved, beautiful, and so adored and appreciated by God, the True Source. As I look back at my practice, I'm amazed and sometimes overwhelmed by the things I do and the love and support I receive from God, the True Source.

Over the years, I have received more gifts and increased enlightenment from God, the True Source. My spiritual classes, intuitive readings, and other types of healing and spiritual workshops have expanded to such an extent that I devote myself full-time to these endeavors. At one point, I met a beautiful woman whom I married. She worked for Boeing and took an early retirement. She convinced me to open up a gift shop with an office in the back for me to do my work. I'll give you one guess as to the gift shop's name. It was called Michael's Angels, and it was located in Kent, Washington.

Many mystical experiences have happened to me since I began teaching. For example, one evening, I had a very prophetic dream in which God, the True Source, told me to start to include soul retrieval in my practice. A week earlier, I had read a book about how Native Americans performed soul retrieval by using their totems. At the time, I had decided that practicing soul retrieval was too arduous, although it made for fascinating reading. In my dream, which seemed very realistic, God, the True Source, told me to start doing soul retrieval because the souls would start coming to me. I argued with God, the True Source, that it was too tenuous and tedious to do soul retrieval. I was told in no uncertain terms that I had done it in past lives and knew all the shortcuts, so I could achieve it quickly and easily. I continued to argue that I would not do it until I woke up. At ten o'clock the next evening, I received a phone call. The caller told me he had gone to see an intuitive in Seattle, and this intuitive, who did not know me, had told him to go see a man named Michael Gross and have a soul retrieval session with him. Reluctantly, I agreed to meet him that evening, and our session lasted until 2 a.m. He had been a captain in the army during the Vietnam Conflict. He also had vague memories from when he was three years old of living in Hawaii when the Japanese bombed Pearl Harbor and strafed his home. Our session was exhausting for me but also very gratifying, and once again, I had powerful spiritual assistance. Since that time, I have done many soul retrievals.

In case you are not familiar with soul retrievals, let me now explain the process. Your over-soul, so to speak, resides in a very highly evolved inner plane also called the spiritual plane. Think of it as your over-soul residing in the bosom of God, the True Source. A part of your over-soul leaves God, the True Source's bosom, and incarnates into an embodiment. On this planet, we call it human embodiment, while it has other names on other planets. This part of your soul, after reviewing its life purpose, karma, and karmic debt, reviews different families and then chooses one that will help it complete its karma, karmic debt, and karma experiences. Once those experiences are completed, one no longer needs to experience them again. As I have said previously, there are two types of karma—one to learn specific lessons and the debts involved with them, and then the positive karma, which has your rewards and positive debts tied to it. When a soul is under extreme stress, no matter what that stress may be, part of your soul fragments and goes into another dimension to hide, heal, be rejuvenated, or any of a myriad of other reasons.

I think it's best here to describe my own personal experience with soul retrieval. It happened when I was in tenth grade and taking a geometry course. My teacher looked to be 150 years old, but being fifteen, anybody close to age sixty or older looked to be 150 years old. Her teaching method was one of intimidation and embarrassment. In the class, she made the boys feel like fools, and she brought the girls to tears. One day, I had forgotten to do my homework; of course, she called on me and embarrassed me. She made an example of me by berating me for at least ten minutes. Later, I would discover that part of my soul had fragmented due to this embarrassing situation. I'll explain how that happened shortly.

Somehow, I still passed the course, but in New York State, where I was going to school, that made no difference because you also had to pass the Regents exam in geometry. The passing grade that year for the Regents exam was 58. I achieved the magnificent score of 50. Obviously, in order to rectify this, I had to go to summer school. In summer school, I had a wonderful teacher who made everything crystal-clear, so when I retook the Regents exam, I scored 98.

Much later, in my thirties, I realized that part of my soul had fragmented due to my embarrassment in that geometry class. The fragment had gone into what I learned later is called a cave, and there it hid out. When I sought out that part of me, I found it (I prefer to refer to it as "him") in a dark cave, embarrassed, sad, and suffering from low self-worth and self-esteem. My soul fragment and I had a conversation, during which I asked him what it would take to remedy the situation. I told him I had gone to summer school to obtain credit for that course. I told him I had received the grade of 98. I reminded him that this experience was in the past, and that I loved him and would respect him. He agreed to come back, and as I felt him coming into my body, a wonderful thing began to change within me. I felt more confident, my self-esteem increased, and I felt full of love, joy, and the zeal to accomplish many things. During soul retrieval, reintegration occurs, which, when done correctly, can be exciting, joyous, and happy!

I have worked with many people since my first soul retrieval, and many magnificent and powerful changes have occurred for those I have helped. They now feel more love, joy, and happiness, and they are leading fruitful, abundant, prosperous, and loving lives. Many of them have also experienced remarkable healings, begun exciting new careers, and had joyful reunions with their families.

"Religion is meant to teach us true spiritual human character. It is meant for self-transformation. It is meant to transform anxiety into peace, arrogance into humility, envy into compassion, to awaken the pure soul in man in his love of the Source, which is God."

— Redhanath Swami

SUMMARY

Remember that on this new journey, you are not alone; you have a huge support team that wants nothing but joy and happiness for you and to make your heart sing. Now is the time to take the leap forward into faith, knowing that in front of you and behind you, there's your full support team and God, the True Source, fully supporting you, fully looking out for you, fully protecting you, and fully helping you to achieve all those things that bring love, joy, and happiness to your life. You are going into the unknown where lie unlimited possibilities to fulfill your heart. Close your eyes and begin your journey. You won't be sorry.

PART III

FAQ's, Affirmations and Thoughts

INTRODUCTION TO FAQ'S, AFFIRMATIONS AND THOUGHTS

"Nothing in life is to be feared, it is only to be understood. Now is the time to understand more, so that we may fear less."

— **Marie Curie**

Beginning your spiritual journey can be scary at first, but there is really nothing to fear. The more you learn, the more you will grow and evolve and become more aligned with your soul. You will experience the truth that you are an aspect of God, the True Source, and desire to continue to learn and become more enlightened.

The way to learn is to ask questions. To facilitate question-asking and growth among those I seek to help, every Tuesday evening, I host a teleseminar to answer questions about spirituality. You may reach me on Tuesday evenings at 6:30 p.m. Pacific by calling 515-739-1020 and entering access code 125446#. The call is completely free to you, other than whatever your long distance provider may or may not charge you.

Following are some of the most frequent and significant questions I am asked and the answers I receive from God, the True Source, in response to them. Remember, these are not my answers. When I am asked a question, I tap into my ability to communicate directly with God, the True Source, to provide these answers.

CHAPTER 15

FREQUENTLY ASKED QUESTIONS

"Do you prefer that you be right, or happy?"

— **A Course in Miracles**

What was Jesus's purpose (mission and goal) on earth?

To understand Jesus and his mission, first we have to understand that this planet was designed to be a true Garden of Eden. But through unintended interference by negative entities and negative energies fostered by jealousy, greed, control, and manipulation, it became necessary for all of the inhabitants on this planet and even in the interdimensional planes to develop a system of protection so we could pursue our missions and goals. The vast majority of this planet at that time was occupied by souls who were experiencing their first and second incarnations and have agreed that one of their missions was to change the planet's consciousness. Because this is a Herculean task, many souls were brought together as a support system. One of the more prominent souls was a special soul who is known by the Hebrew name of Joshua Ben Yosef, or in English, Jesus son of Joseph.

Jesus was born into a wealthy family composed of excellent woodworkers and business people. He was not born in a barn, but rather in a cave that is marked clearly in Israel as his birthplace. His birth was kept secret to protect him from King Herod, who feared that if a new king were born, he would be replaced. According to Matthew 2:16-18:

> When Herod realized that he had been deceived by the Magi, he became furious. He ordered the massacre of all the boys of Bethlehem and its vicinity two years old and under, in accordance with the time he had ascertained from the Magi. Then was fulfilled what had been said to Jeremiah the prophet:
> "a voice was heard in Ramah,
> sobbing and loud lamentation;
> Rachel weeping for her children,
> and she would not be consoled,
> since they were no more."

This event became known as the Massacre of the Innocents. Fortunately, Joseph had a dream warning him of the possible murder of his son, so the family fled to Egypt. There Joseph practiced his trade and obtained moderate financial success. He had long ago realized from visions and prophecies revealed to him in dreams that Jesus had a special role to play.

One day, the Pharaoh's son was diagnosed with leprosy. Jesus, at a very young age, was able to cure him. As a result, Joseph's family was given luxurious quarters to live in and much wealth. Eventually,

Joseph had another dream telling him to return with his family back to Israel because King Herod had died.

Jesus began his training after the family returned home. What are known as the "lost years" of Jesus's life were spent as he trained with Hindus, Buddhists, Druids, and many other groups who had established schools of spiritual education called "mystery schools." Great spirituality was taught in these schools, and it was practiced by a select few advanced souls. Proof exists that Jesus was taught at the various schools in the form of drawings on stone in Hindu temples and other locations. One well-known practice among those highly evolved spiritual souls who attended the mystery schools—which by the way, still exist today—is the ability to leave the human body for almost a week or longer and then come back into the body to rejuvenate it. Much mysticism and spiritual knowledge was taught to Jesus during this time. The gospel stories of the miracles Jesus performed—miraculous healings, manifestation of food, etc.—were commonly achieved by the schools' students; Jesus learned to perform such miracles there. Through his studies, he was able to align himself to be an instrument of God, the True Source, so he could accomplish his mission. It is important to note, however, that Jesus was already an advanced soul and had the innate ability to embrace and facilitate the mystery schools' teaching.

By Jesus's time, the Hebrews had become so distant from their original practices that they were becoming lost and consumed by greed, especially the Jewish leaders. Jesus's mission was to change the consciousness of all those who would listen to him so they could reconnect to God, the True Source. While he mostly preached to the Hebrews (Israelites or Jews), he also taught and preached to others.

Before his crucifixion, Jesus married Mary Magdalene. It was ordained that he would take on the negative karma of the Israelites so they would be free to pursue their spirituality without any negative karma for their race. Over time, the Hebrews' karma began to change. It is a common practice by some swamis and others to take on negative karma; in the process, they leave their bodies for a period of time to embrace, heal, and release the negative karma. Jesus, in his great love for the Israelites, took it upon himself to take on, in embodiment, their negative karma in order to free them. While on the cross, Jesus began the process of leaving his body for this purpose. By leaving his body, he was able to feel no pain. By the time they removed him from the cross and placed him in a tomb, he was still out of his body. During that time, his life force appeared to be nonexistent, resembling a death state. When the women came to wash his body three days later, Jesus was nowhere to be found. He had come back into his body, healed his body, and begun the long process of achieving his mission and goal by traveling all over the world to enlighten souls to reconnect to God, the True Source.

The New Testament reports that Jesus told his disciples they would be able to do all the things he had done and even greater, and he even explained the stars, the moon, and parts of the universe to them. After his "resurrection," Jesus, incognito, left with his wife Mary Magdalene and their two children to live in France. A secret order of men was created to protect Mary Magdalene and their children. As the children grew, it was felt that their future generations were the legal heirs to the Catholic Church. In order to protect them and the future generations to come, there were those who dedicated their lives to protecting Jesus, Mary Magdalene, and their children. This group of dedicated men and women eventually evolved into the Knights Templar. While Mary and their children were protected by these loving men and women in France, Jesus went on many other travels. Stories exist of him being in South America and also visiting the Native Americans in North America.

The Knights Templar are known for having protected the descendants of both Jesus and Mary, but the Catholic Church always assumed that they were protecting the family of Mary, Jesus's mother, not Mary Magdalene. In the early fourteenth century, when Pope Clement V found out it was the offspring of Mary Magdalene (Jesus's children) who were being protected, he and King Philip IV of France decided to annihilate the Knights Templar. Because the Knights Templar believed Jesus's descendants were the true heirs to the seat of the Catholic Church, they were perceived as a threat to the papacy. Despite the destruction of the Knights Templar, Jesus's bloodline still exists today. If we accept that Jesus lived 2,000 years ago, then it is clear that the descendants of Jesus's children would have expanded exponentially. As a result, the number of people who carry his bloodline is incredibly huge—in the millions if not the billions.

Whether you accept this version of Jesus's life is up to you as an individual. While much that is fictional has been written about Jesus, there are books that document the facts and go into great detail. For example, in *He Walked the Americas*, Lucille Taylor Hansen explored the idea that Jesus traveled to the Americas and visited the indigenous peoples there. Hansen is an anthropologist, archaeologist, and geologist. For more than forty years, she collected and compiled stories from Native American oral histories. These stories all spoke of a "fair-skinned, bearded prophet" who spoke thousands of languages, healed the sick, raised the dead, and taught in the same words Jesus is reported to have used in the gospels. Although Jesus was referred to by different names according to different tribes' languages, all the stories describe him in the same manner as a tall, bearded man wearing white robes. There is a story that when Jesus went to the Temple Ek Balaam in Guatemala, the high priest threatened Jesus and called him a demon. When Jesus raised his palms before him, the high priest saw in each one a large cross torn in the flesh. The high priest stood as one transfixed. The story goes that Jesus then spoke to a man of that tribe named Kee-Chee, saying he brought a message from the God who has no image. He talked to Kee-Chee and his people about the two paths they could take. One was the path of evil and one was the path of God. He explained the commandment to "Love one another." It is said that Jesus walked from tribe to tribe among the American nations, and he came to Peru from the Pacific. Then he traveled through South and Central America among the Mayans, into Mexico, and then all of North America, then back to the ancient Tula, from whence he departed across the Atlantic to his land of origin. Personally, I believe the information Hansen collected is overwhelmingly accurate. Many other books on the topic have also been written that make it difficult not to believe that Jesus visited many countries in the Americas, Asia, and Europe. Judge for yourself!

Why are there so many different religions?

Let's use the concept of a wagon wheel to understand this topic. A wagon wheel that has many spokes, all the spokes lead to the small circle known as the hub. We can use this analogy to understand there are many different paths represented by the spokes that will achieve reconnection with God, the True Source. The spokes all end up encircling the hub, which is a metaphor representing God, the True Source. It is important for each person to realize there are many different paths to arrive at the same point and you must be open to the path that resonates with you. I believe God, the True Source, has designated me to illustrate the quickest path and one of least resistance to reconnecting with God, the True Source. That is part of my mission and goal on this earthly plane. The decision to choose a path and reconnect lies deep within the soul of each individual person.

In my early days before embarking on my spiritual path of enlightenment, I asked God, the True Source: Why are there so many religions and what is religion's purpose? The answer I received was that most religions set up a moral code (some of which have been bastardized, changed, or manipulated for specific controlling reasons) in order to create a balance of some type. True spiritual seekers realize there is something beyond the religions they have chosen to experience; that realization is their first step toward enlightenment and understanding. Almost all religions state their way is the only way to reconnect to God, the True Source. What we truly need to do is to focus, like the wagon wheel does on the hub, which is a metaphor for God, the True Source, and also a metaphor for the Truth Source and for God, the True Source's Unconditional Love. If the collective consciousness on Earth focuses on God, the True Source's energy of unconditional love, allowing, and non-judgmentalness, then everything and everyone will now change in a most powerful way to that energy. Think about this: If each one of us focuses on unconditional love and allowingness, aligning ourselves with the energy of God, the True Source, then our mass consciousness will change this planet into a positive loving Garden of Eden, just as it was originally designed to be—a place of love, healing, en-lightenment, joy, and complete oneness with God, the True Source. I charge each one of you to rely upon your Inner Guidance from God, the True Source, to take on this challenge of changing this planet into the Garden of Eden to bring about a mass conscious-ness of unconditional love! This is the time when we must all pull together to achieve this Herculean task. We are at a great crossroads where mass consciousness could go into darkness or into light! You now have a golden opportunity to end war, greed, famine, illness, poverty, and far, far greater inadequacies upon this planet. Choose wisely, for it is incumbent upon *you* to be that positive change! Now that you have awoken from your long slumber by reading this book, you know you have a great ally, *God, the True Source!* I now charge *you* to be that change! You are unlimited!

Are individuals the products of their DNA, their souls, or both, and if both, is it fifty-fifty?

This question is highly important because its answer will also answer many of the other questions we have. As I've said previously, each person who reincarnates from God, the True Source, has mis-sions and goals on both the human and spiritual planes.

Before we incarnate, we choose our family for some specific reasons. Some of these reasons have to do with our family's DNA since it will fit with our missions and goals. Perhaps an individual will choose to be tall and imposing so the message he has to deliver will be listened to. Or perhaps, like Mohammed Ali, he chooses to reincarnate as a boxer to achieve fame but also to be revered for his many spiritual quotes. In a previous life, Mohammed Ali had been a great warrior in Sparta, which, as you know, is the warrior sect of

Greece. In his most recent lifetime, he chose to have a similarly athletic body so he could experience great success and simultaneously bring respect and fame to his race. He also championed people of other races, as evidenced by his friendship with the Jewish sports announcer, Howard Cosell. This behavior helped to accomplish his mission and goals.

Others choose their families' DNA for karmic reasons in relation to their missions and goals. For example, when I was the sales manager for a company, I had to hire another salesman, who had an excellent track record. When I interviewed him, he disclosed to me that no male in his family had ever lived beyond age forty-two. Since he was forty at the time, he wanted me to be aware of this fact. While I did not have a problem with it, the corporation did, so unfortunately, I could not hire him. Later, I found out that he had died at age forty-two. Years later, I learned that he had chosen his family for its DNA, realizing that he would have a relatively short life in which to accomplish his mission and goals. By the time of his death, he had accomplished them.

Others may choose the DNA of a frail person so they can experience love, support, compassion, etc. What is important to remember is that you are not your DNA; rather, we are all souls, here to experience life, heal our karma and karmic debt, fulfill our missions and goals, and be role models to one another other.

What is the correlation between our soul and the oversoul?

The best way to answer this question is for you to understand your connection to God, the True Source. In the Judeo-Christian religions, it is stated that we are made in the "Image of God." This is another way of saying we are an "Aspect of God, the True Source." In essence, we are part of "God, the True Source."

The best way to illustrate this is by using a simple analogy. Just as you and your children have the DNA of yourself or your parents, figuratively speaking, the DNA or essence of God, the True Source, is you! Therefore, God, the True Source, is part of you, and conversely, you are part of God, the True Source.

There is a part of you, your aspect of God, the True Source, that is separate yet intertwined in oneness with God, the True Source. That part of you is called the "oversoul." The oversoul resides in the, figuratively speaking, bosom of God, the True Source. A part of the oversoul, which I now call our "bodily soul," leaves and on this planet joins and becomes one with the fetus. The bodily soul, now in the fetus, proceeds on its chosen life path in order to learn, grow, heal, and experience karma/karmic debt. The bodily soul's life path has been previously agreed upon and encoded into it before its incarnation. The bodily soul's role of the fetus is always to be in communication with the oversoul for several purposes, including to remind it of its missions and goals in this lifetime and share its experiences from the bodily soul to the oversoul and on into God, the True Source. In this way, God, the True Source, vicariously understands the experience that each soul is having.

It is important to understand that God, the True Source, has only one energy, frequency, and vibration that is unconditional love. It is pure and can never be tainted. All the experiences we have in our life, whether positive or negative, by our judgment, we have created or allowed to be created in order to grow and learn and experience. There is more about this in my book about the Twelve Spiritual Laws. At the end of our current lifetime, the bodily soul and oversoul unite and prepare themselves for another incarnation or type of spiritual work that could include another incarnation, or becoming a celestial being, or energetically working on the spiritual plane for certain goals or other creative purposes.

I have been asked whether the soul in embodiment ever meets the oversoul in embodiment. The answer is no. That is because they are different vibrations, frequencies, and energies, and have different work to do, as I have previously explained.

I have also been asked whether the oversoul can have different parts of itself incarnate simultaneously. The answer is, of course, yes. It depends upon what the oversoul desires to accomplish in order for it to grow. Therefore, the oversoul cannot only incarnate in this dimension and planet multiple times, but also in other universes and dimensions. It is also possible that the bodily soul, which has split itself into other parts, could meet itself. I have never heard of this happening, but I'm told there is a very, very slight possibility it could.

If we stop to think about this, you can now realize and understand that we are never alone, and you are always connected to God, the True Source. If you desire to, take time to center yourself and block out your mind chatter and you will always learn what direction you need to follow. I call this, God, the True Source's Inner Guidance. There are directions in this book on how to meditate and prepare yourself for this guidance. After reading how to do it, my suggestion is to apply it and ask to receive God, the True Source's Inner Guidance.

Is it important for us to know our past lives and bring the knowledge and skills from those lives into this lifetime?

Having done many past life regressions, I know that many people want to know whether in previous lifetimes they were famous or were kings or queens, etc. The truth is that it is not important whether you were a king, queen, or president. What you were in your past life does not change what you came to accomplish in this incarnation; however, your past life does affect your present. As an old geometric equation states, the sum of the parts equals the whole. In other words, the gifts you are experiencing and the goals you are accomplishing in this lifetime are an accumulation of all your past lifetimes. Whether you were a coal miner or a potentate in the past does make a difference because those qualities are brought into this lifetime to help you fulfill the missions and goals you have chosen in this lifetime.

Have you ever observed that some people are natural carpenters, artists, healers, or leaders? That is because they have done those things in previous lifetimes and are now applying their past skills to this lifetime. God, the True Source, shared a beautiful quote with me on this topic: *"I am not my body. I am not my past. I am. I am you. You are me. We are one."* I believe that says it all.

Do we reincarnate upon the same planet?

Sometimes a soul may choose to reincarnate upon the same planet based on its karma. Or it may go into other universes or other forms or other dimensions in order to grow. It is important to remember that each one of us chooses which experiences we desire to have in order to grow. Our vibrational frequencies and energies' purpose, sometimes called our heart's strongest desire, is to get back into the bosom of God, the True Source. The only way this can be done is if we ourselves are truly and unequivocally unconditionally loving, allowing ourselves to be nonjudgmental just like God, the True Source. Until that time, we choose to work our way back into that energy. Once we do so, we are united in oneness—with the vibrational frequency and energy—with God, the True Source. There comes a time when we are either bored or have been asked to take on a new mission and goal and begin the reincarnation process all over again. That is the sacrifice we intentionally partake in to help all humanity, all entities, and all souls, no matter what vibrations, frequencies, or planes they reside in, to accomplish reconnection at the highest level possible to God, the True Source. As I have said previously in this book, our DNA in this embodiment is also natural to this planet and at the same time foreign to it. Take into consideration that our DNA consists of many alien races due to intentional and unintentional crossbreeding.

Can a person or animal's passing on to the higher realms be delayed by another person's grieving or desire not to let go?

Firstly, it is believed that it takes approximately nine days after a person's death to make the full transition to the other side and return to the bosom of God, the True Source. While that is the standard, some souls are able to go more quickly based on their past lives and higher vibrations. Most souls grieve not for their loved ones but for their loss. It is this grieving and not willing to let go, either from guilt, loss, or some other reason, that can slow the deceased person's transition to the other side. When you grieve, the deceased person or animal has great compassion and love for you. By grieving, you create a tie with your loved one that makes the person want to be around you until you have reached the point where you can let go. In my understanding, there is no specific timeframe; it could take moments or years. Is it not wonderful to understand how much compassion and love our loved ones have for us that they will not leave our side until we are ready to let them go? However, it is important to realize that they must move on and that we do not have the spiritual right to block their growth; they also need time to heal and later reincarnate. As a suggestion, you might go into a meditative state and ask permission to speak with your loved one's soul. Whether you receive conscious permission or not, proceed to tell your loved one how much you miss and love him or her, what joy he or she brought into your life, as well as anything else you wish to share. You will be honoring your loved one and his or her life path through this process. It will also accomplish three important goals: 1) it frees your loved one to move on, 2) it frees you to move on, and 3) it allows you to heal physically, mentally, and emotionally, perhaps even preventing some kind of serious illness in your life.

While letting go of a deceased loved one may be difficult, it is a very powerful, loving, positive, and karmic thing to do. Your loved one will appreciate the love, emotions, and forgiveness you extend and will extend the same to you; it is reciprocal. Once you have let go, rest assured that you will be hearing from your loved one either through your dreams, a message in your thoughts, or something that reminds you of him or her when you least expect it. Your loved ones who have passed on will always try to communicate with you to say they are all right and on a grand positive journey. Unfortunately, sometimes our sadness or anxiety blocks messages they are trying to send to us. Be mindful that these messages are being sent, but do not have expectations for them because that creates anxiety, which will block them. When you least expect it, something will occur out of the blue to lift your heart and soul and let you know your loved one is just fine.

Why is there so much fear on this planet?

To answer this question, it is important to understand the conveyance of energy to human beings. As previously explained, we are all comprised of energies vibrating at different frequencies and levels. One frequency we vibrate at is that of emotional energy. We are like a sponge picking up on different variations of energies, which in turn affect our physical, mental, and emotional bodies. It is as if we each have a large antenna that is picking up and responding to various energies while at the same time broadcasting our own energies that we call feelings and emotions. These feelings and emotions can be best explained as anxiety, fear, insecurity, frustration, depression, and hate, as well as joy, happiness, and exhilaration.

This understanding begs the question: What is it about humans that allows them to be unaware or in denial of their connection to God, the True Source? Perhaps the answer is that they doubt or do not believe that they are aspects of God, the True Source. In Western culture, we are taught scientific methods, including that if we cannot see it, smell it, touch it, taste it, or hear it, then it does not exist. Yet if we look at all the beauty in this world—trees, flowers, the landscape, the sunrise and sunset, the oceans, mountains, and also the charity and love of so many souls—it is clear that something beautiful and mysterious is going on in this world that reflects our thoughts, feelings, and emotions.

Has someone ever said to you, "Wow, you look happier," or "You look good today," or some other positive comment about your demeanor? Can you remember how that remark made you feel even happier? Or perhaps someone said, "You look sick," or "You look tired," or something not so flattering. Did you observe your energy beginning to drop as you took on the feelings that resulted from what that person said to you? These are but a few examples of how other people's energies and the planet's energies can affect us. A few other examples include feeling an impending storm coming or perhaps intuitively feeling that something was going to go awry in your life or that it was your lucky day.

One time, I was in Aruba at a casino when a person I was with told me, "This is my lucky slot machine." We were there for several days, and I observed that at the very time he had said that, he would always win the jackpot. I realized that he was manifesting this luck unintentionally but very successfully. As an experiment, I decided to do the same thing. I brought forth energy that said, "This is my lucky slot machine and I'm going to win." Then I placed one dollar in, but nothing occurred. However, with the second dollar I inserted, I won the jackpot which was in excess of $500. This experiment proves that the energy you put forth in your thoughts and emotions affects everything around you; even if you're expressing it to an inanimate object, the outcome will reflect whatever you are thinking or feeling.

It is wonderful to realize that when you are in harmony and balance with the Divine's energy, all things are possible. Through my experiments, I learned that the Divine desires me to be prosperous and to enjoy life. This realization was a great aha moment in my life. As long as you do not worship money or prosperity, and you trust by letting go and letting God, the True Source, all things desirable and needed in your life in order for you to feel fulfilled—no matter what they are—will be automatically provided for you. So get out of your way and let it happen. It is important once you make a request that you get out of your own way; do not try to control how it will be given to you; just know it will happen at the most perfect and opportune time in your life! This is part of the key!

If you want to know the other keys to manifestation, go back and reread the chapter in Part I on the Law of Manifestation. I suggest you reread it and reread it until you fully understand, embrace, and practice the Law of Manifestation. Remember, your only limitations are self-imposed! You are the major creator of your life. There are no victims, only unenlightened and frightened souls stuck in life by their own fears, doubts, lack of self-worth, lack of self-esteem, lack of love, lack of joy, and lack of happiness. Pure unadulterated logic will tell you that since you are an aspect of God, the True Source, all positive things are possible. Think about this for a moment: You are an aspect of the Divine; would the Divine desire anything less than all the best for itself? Remember, you and God, the True Source, are one.

Is there a hell?

There is no such thing as hell! The word hell came from the Hebrew word for garbage dump. If one could not afford a proper burial place, the only place available to use was the garbage dump. The same applies to the word "sin," which in Hebrew means "missed the mark." Modern religions have chosen hell as a way to control and manipulate souls for certain political and financial religious gains. Stop for a minute and ask yourself: If God, the True Source, is unconditionally loving, allowing, and nonjudgmental, why would there be a hell? Recently, I read that Pope Francis stated in a conversation with a friend that there is no such thing as hell. What a great revelation! That is true. Therefore, you are probably asking: What happens when a person does negative things? The answer is so simplistic and yet very powerful. Through God, the True Source's wisdom, each soul has decided that responsibility had to be taken for everything the soul has experienced or created that is not loving. That is when the concept of karma/karmic debt was created. In simplistic terms, karma is nothing but an experience. Therefore, when negativity is created, each soul will experience it in this lifetime or future lifetimes in order never to create the negativity again. But since karma/karmic debt applies equally and all things that one has created must be experienced, all the loving things done in a lifetime that encompasses joy (e.g., sharing prosperity, healing, love, and other things we have shared with others) are also to be experienced. The concept is rewarding and empowering; whether you think it is negative or positive is immaterial. Remember, karma/karmic debt is nothing but an experience. Our missions and goals on the human plane and on the spiritual plane are all part of what we have chosen to experience to share and grow. Think for a moment how powerful and wonderful this concept is. Those souls that remain negative and refuse to accept love are quarantined until they are ready to accept the frequency, vibration, and energy of God, the True Source's Love. Once they do, they go through a series of levels (dimensions, frequencies, and vibrations) to work their way back to reincarnate, realizing their karma/debt has to be made right.

Does God, the True Source, really judge us?

The answer is an emphatic: No! When a soul births out of its physical body, it goes to a plane where it has a life review. It then feels the energy of everything it has ever done and the emotion of everyone it has ever affected. It makes no difference whether it is positive or negative, the soul feels that emotion. During this process, the soul is surrounded by celestial beings (I call them God, the True Source's Created Resources), also known as guides, master guides, angels, guardian angels, archangels, etc. They are there to support and love the soul and help it understand its experiences. No judgment is made. Perhaps you are wondering why? As I have said before, God, the True Source, is unconditionally loving, allowing, and nonjudgmental. The Law of Karma helps illustrate what experiences each one of us has chosen to have in order to grow, learn, and move forward.

How do we learn what our karma is and how do we release our karmic debt?

Meditate and ask God, the True Source, to help you experience and know what is your karma and karmic debt. Once you are able to ascertain what they are, ask to experience them fully and deeply; then ask to release them and be healed. You must do this exercise completely. Do not try to fool yourself because when you do it properly, you will feel the release. Once you complete it, there will no longer be any blocks or encumbrances upon you in this life or in future lives because your soul will only desire to go back to the bosom of God, the True Source. Until that is achieved, karmic lessons have to be cleansed, healed, and cleared in as many lifetimes as it takes.

As I've pointed out before, everything you do in this or any other incarnation is a karmic experience. Therefore, if you were to give away millions of dollars in this lifetime, then you would have to experience what it is like to receive millions of dollars in another lifetime. On the other hand, your karma might be something negative that also needs to be cleared. After reviewing the karmic lessons you have chosen to experience, God, the True Source's created resources—a.k.a., guides, master guides, guardian angels, and other angels—will make sure you're not too hard on yourself. They will then work with you to help you find a balance.

The next thing that must be decided is what family you choose to have assist you in your karmic experiences. Because you have had multiple incarnations, you have a large spiritual family, and you tend to incarnate with those family members so that they will be your parents, children, siblings, other relatives, or friends in a lifetime. Let us say that in a past life or lives, you had low self-worth, self-esteem, and self-love. You would most likely choose a family that would either be loving so you could heal that karma, or perhaps you wish to experience that situation more in-depth so you can acquire what is necessary for you to learn. Therefore, you choose a family that has addiction problems or is impoverished. Once you birth into your chosen family, the "veil of forgetfulness," for the most part, descends upon you. The veil of forgetfulness is exactly that, causing each experience in your new lifetime to be something new for you.

The beautiful part about this human experience is that once you learn the karmic lesson you have chosen with others assisting you, unknowingly you begin the process of eliminating more and more karmic lessons you had acquired over many past lifetimes. At the same time, karma also applies to those you closely interact with— for example, friends, family members, lovers, relatives, and teachers. This explains why some souls have chosen very difficult incarnations while others have had relatively easy ones. Remember that we have free will and free choice before we incarnate and even afterwards, so everything we experience is something we intend to use to learn and grow from. Even the most difficult incarnations and lessons you have chosen are for the purpose to become more enlightened, to raise your vibrations to accomplish your mission and goal, and as to reconnect directly with God, the True Source.

While we're on the subject of reincarnation, I want to explain that you bring forth many tools (knowledge) and gifts from previous lifetimes in order to achieve your goals in this lifetime. You also make agreements with other souls, whose incarnations will overlap with your lifetime, to assist one another in the karmic growth and experiences you have chosen. That is one side of the coin, so to speak. The other side is, as I've mentioned before, you have your missions and goals to accomplish on the human and spiritual planes. Therefore, you will act with others as a team to assist one another in your important missions and goals.

Perhaps you are wondering why you are born with the veil of forgetfulness. The answer is both complex and simple. If you knew we were here just to experience life and heal our karmic debt and lessons, then if you chose not to achieve that, you could be very blasé about it and decide just to come back as often as you needed so that you may eventually heal and clear your karmic lessons (experiences). It would then take a long time for you to clear and heal the karma, which would delay your journey of reconnection with your "over-soul," which resides in oneness with God, the True Source. As stated previously, your "over-soul" resides with God, the True Source, but a portion of it incarnates into your body, or multiple bodies if you so desire, to heal your karma more quickly and help you accomplish your multiple missions and goals. In any given incarnation, you could actually incarnate into as many as eight different bodies, in different dimensions and universes.

Is it wrong to be rich or prosperous?

This question is really one about which belief systems are correct. It came from a person who told me he was quite confused about prosperity because his family had taught him that you only need enough money to fulfill your basic needs, and if you had anything extra, you should give it away or share it with others. He added that at times his family had struggled while at other times they had

had more than enough. He related to me that one month he had been incredibly financially prosperous to the point that he felt over-whelming guilt because of the abundance of money he earned. The following month, his business began to subside. I explained to him that the belief system he had received from his family had become his modus operandi. He had created prosperity and abundance for one month, and then through guilt, he had created the opposite.

I explained to him that every thought is a manifestation, every word is a manifestation, and every action is a manifestation, so as you think, so shall you create. As I have said before, all thoughts are electromagnetic, meaning whatever you think, you magnetize and draw to you. The universe does not judge whether what you think about is positive or negative; it only delivers to you what you think about, thus creating it in your life. I further explained to him that everything that exists is an aspect of God, the True Source, and that God, the True Source, desires all of us to experience everything at all levels. We, in turn, through vibrational frequencies and energy, telepathically share our experiences with both God, the True Source, and everyone around us, including, but not limited to, our family, friends, and relatives. Since the Divine Spirit (God, the True Source) has created or co-created with you everything that exists, why would the Divine Spirit not want you to bring forth anything and everything that brings unlimited joy, happiness, perfect health, perfection, etc.?

Therefore, it is important for each of you to realize that anything and everything is available to you to experience so long as it does not become your "false god" to worship. The true test in knowing whether you worship money or anything else that comes into your life through manifestation is whether you are fearful that you will lose what you have created. I pointed out to this person that if you have manifested something once, you can manifest it over and over and over again. Therefore, let nothing own you, and realize that whatever you create in your life is to be created for the purposes of joy, happiness, and the sheer experience of it.

In this person's particular case, the prosperity he created was something he chose to experience, and perhaps it was a positive and karmic experience for him to learn about growth, spirituality, manifestation, and being unlimited through the creation and then experience the loss of that prosperity through his guilt. He had not realized his guilt was another manifestation. Therein lies the true secret of manifestation—being unlimited and knowing that it is your birthright to create everything you so desire to experience. An old proverb states, "Argue for your limitations and you own them." This leads us to our next question.

How can we be sure we are manifesting correctly and not self-sabotaging ourselves?

As I said earlier, 94 percent of our thinking comes from our subconscious/unconscious mind while 6 percent comes from our conscious mind. You may wonder how scientists came to that conclusion. They did an experiment using a device called an electro-encephalogram (EEG), which measures brain waves and identifies repetitive thought patterns. Several thoughts were verbally placed into the mind via hypnotherapy. Then the study's volunteers were connected to the EEG. The scientists observed the volunteers' sleep thought patterns and later their thought patterns while awake. This observation demonstrated that the same thought pattern is repeated over and over again. The end result was that whichever thoughts we have consciously expressed do not repeat themselves or at least not as strongly. Those coming from the subconscious/ unconscious mind have a stronger connection and are repeated more frequently. Those repetitive subconscious thoughts begin to overtake and block the conscious thoughts, and thus, they manifest into your life.

Many people are unaware that the subconscious mind recreates a thought over and over again. This repetition can be very positive and assist you in creating wonderful accomplishments in your life or it can be negative and block many of your desires. Remember, the universe does not judge; only we judge, based on the learning curve we had when we were born and in our early learning environments with parents, our extended family, religious teachers, educational teachers, etc. The patterns and behaviors we develop during this time follow us for the rest of our lives unless we become aware of them and change them.

Thoughts, whether positive or negative, come in one of two ways: 1) through constant repetition, or 2) through a type of deep jolting energy; for example, being scolded, being yelled at, or by receiving severe criticism or enthusiastic praise. Your subconscious/unconscious mind thinks only in black and white, or only in positive or negative; there is no gray area or deductive reasoning. Fortunately, the conscious mind does look at information as black, white, or gray. That is why affirmations, which are consciously repeated, will change the subconscious and conscious minds into achieving the desired result. It is also important to remember that we cannot have two simultaneous thoughts. A thought is either positive or negative, but not a combination of both. Once you are in control of your life and your thoughts, you become the sole (soul) creator of anything you desire to bring into your life to experience. Remember, everything is temporal in this life, and you are the unlimited creator of it.

Before we move on to the next question, let's take time to do an exercise to look at our belief system.

EXERCISE

What negative beliefs do you hold about yourself, others, or life in general that may be holding you back from experiencing happiness?

_____

_____

_____

_____

_____

How have your negative beliefs controlled your life?

_____

_____

_____

_____

_____

What are you going to do to change them?

_____

_____

_____

_____

_____

To change your beliefs, I suggest you begin to focus and meditate on these two mantras:

- "I am created out of love; therefore, I am loved."
- "I am one with God, the True Source, and God, the True Source, is one with me."

I would like you first to meditate on the first affirmation. The essence of Divine Spirit is pure unadulterated, unconditional love. Everything that God, the True Source, creates is done with pure unconditional love. By meditating on that thought, you will eventually come to the realization that everything created out of pure unconditional love is perfect in each and every way. It is only we humans who place limitations, fears, or doubts on those thoughts.

The next affirmation affirms your sole (soul) connection to the Divine, which is immutable and has always been permanent. Since the Divine is pure unconditional love and loves you as a parent loves his or her children, the Divine desires everything for you that brings you love, joy, and happiness.

It is imperative that you believe everything is possible to fulfill your life. Reciting the above mantras will help you reach that level of belief. By repeating the above mantras at least thirty-six times per day, you will begin to notice your life changing in very positive ways. You will realize that something magical is taking place with your dreams and hopes. The next step will be witnessing your dreams and hopes as they become your reality.

Remember the story of Perseus. He fought Medusa, whose hair was composed of multiple snakes, and whose stare could turn men into stone. To protect himself, he raised up his shield so he could not look at her. When she looked at him, the shininess of his shield caused her to see her reflection, which caused the energy from her eyes to bounce off the shield and turn her into stone. Whether this story is fact or fiction, it illustrates how energy projected toward our reflection will return to us a hundredfold. Therefore, I recommend that when you recite the two affirmations above, you do so in front of a mirror to make things happen more quickly. It is said that if you repeat a mantra for forty days, it becomes firmly embedded in your energy fields and consciousness, thus creating the desired result. I firmly believe this is true; therefore, I strongly suggest you try it. What have you got to lose? If you find yourself becoming resistant, could it be because of your ego or some issues of worthiness?

Why do we have to have karmic experiences if we have free will and free choice?

Before you incarnate, you have a life review of your past lives and then you choose the proper life for you. The karmic experiences that you selected will help you benefit and grow in your next life. You are not forced to have these experiences; it's a choice. Therefore, you may take on as little or as much as you desire. God, the True Source's created resources make sure that you are not too hard on yourself and only select those karmic experiences you can individually handle. You also know before you incarnate that you will not take this journey alone because God, the True Source's created resources will be there to assist you in learning your lessons. Once you incarnate, the process begins. If, during your incarnation, you choose only to have some of the experiences you previously chose, you can learn and grow from those and experience the others in future lifetimes to continue the karmic lesson/experiences. In other words, your agreements are revocable. However, if you so choose, you can make your karmic lessons irrevocable, which is what I did. (I think spirit gave me lots of champagne and caviar to make me drunk while I signed the agreement to make it irrevocable.) I was told that because of my challenges in this lifetime, I might not complete my mission and goal unless I had made it irrevocable.

You are probably wondering what additional reasons would cause soul to make their karmic agreements irrevocable? Because the soul is afraid that during the incarnation he or she may back out, and the soul knows how important it is to learn that karmic lesson, so the soul does not want to leave any room for human weakness to interfere. Personally, I have often wondered why I made certain of my karmic lessons irrevocable. I eventually realized this decision was made with a great deal of wisdom and was the correct decision for me. Not that there haven't been many times in this lifetime when I've wanted to say, "Scotty, beam me up!" But that's all the more reason why I made them irrevocable. Ultimately, I desire to fulfill my mission in this lifetime to help all who will listen to reconnect with God, the True Source, heal this planet, and change the mass consciousness to one of unconditional love.

Where does inspiration come from? Is it true that some people can receive inspiration from a higher source?

By the grace and love of God, the True Source, there is a place on the spiritual/inner plane in a specifically designated area where everything that has ever been thought of, conceived, dreamt, or conceptualized has been collected and stored. This place is called the "Universal Band of Knowledge." It contains not only what applies to Mother Earth and its inhabitants, but what applies to the whole universe and all of its inhabitants. Just think—all the knowledge that has been placed in the span over billions of years is stored there. Perhaps you can liken it to accessing information from your computer into the space called the "Cloud." To me, this is literally mind-boggling.

At the turn of the last century, Nikola Tesla conceived ideas that were way beyond the knowledge of humans on planet earth during his incarnation. He created free energy as well as the AC current. He made many other discoveries and inventions too numerous to mention here. Most believe he was ahead of his time, which, no doubt, he was. However, what he was able to do was access the Universal Band of Knowledge to create his numerous inventions so he could assist humanity. Regretfully, he did not patent his inventions because he felt they should be made available to all freely. Much to his chagrin, they were stolen by others for greedy purposes. I suggest you research his life story if you wish to know more about him.

Albert Einstein was also able to access the Universal Band Knowledge. In his early years, he took only a portion of that knowledge and intellectually expanded upon it. Later, he went back to review some of his theories and realized he had been wrong in some instances; the reason he was wrong was because in his excitement, he did not take time to obtain the entire information. He later postulated new theories that turned out to be more accurate, which, to some extent, we are only finding out now.

Many times throughout history, individuals have thought about creating new concepts, devices, etc., and have unintentionally begun to access information from the Universal Band of Knowledge. Some of those items have to do with computers, cell phones, battery-operated cars, and engines. The Universal Band of Knowledge is not for a select few, but rather for anyone who desires to access it. As we look about our world today, we can see that more and more technology is appearing, and most of this new technology comes from those creative individuals who have been inadvertently accessing the Universal Band of Knowledge.

By now, I have peaked your interest, so you are probably wondering whether you could do the same. The answer is: Yes, of course! The easiest way to access any information you desire is to place yourself in a meditative state. To obtain more information on how to do this, you may email me through my website at www. DrMichaelGross.com. I will then share with you the correct protocol for consciously obtaining this information. There is one caveat; the information you seek must be good for all of humankind.

Your next question may be: What information can I obtain? The answer is anything and everything—music, poetry, literature, scientific information, etc. Just use your creative thoughts and ask for what you seek to learn and know. You will be amazed by what information you are able to glean. Once you have achieved this, realize you can go back and back again to obtain the same or more information. I suggest that since you have received this information freely, you should seriously consider sharing it with everyone rather than doing what some of the early pioneers and corporations have done, which is using it only for self-serving profitable reasons. In terms of sharing this information, all I can say is to let your conscience, soul, and higher self be your guide. It is also important that you acknowledge where this information came from: always be sure to give thanks to God, the True Source, for being allowed the privilege of obtaining it.

I've heard about something called the Akashic records. Can you explain what those are?

In essence, the Akashic records is a history of your life beginning from the moment you left the bosom of God, the True Source, to this very moment. Everything you have ever accomplished, everything you have ever done mistakenly, everyone you have ever hurt, everyone you have ever brought joy and happiness to, and everything you have ever experienced is recorded in these records. This information includes your current mission and goal in human and spiritual planes. The purpose of the Akashic Records is for you to understand what karmic lessons you have learned and how much you have changed and grown. At the end of your life, when you have birthed (transitioned) out of your body, you have a life review. This review explores your missions, goals, and karmic lessons from your past lives so you can prepare for your next life. The practice of this review explains, for the most part, why and how we choose to live and do what we do, such as become lawyers, doctors, carpenters, company presidents, leaders, heads of state, parents, caretakers, etc. It also explains why some souls have addictions or mental impairments or are paraplegic, autistic, or have other maladies. I mention those who experience these challenges because it is important for us to honor these souls and have great compassion for them because they have chosen huge monumental challenges to help them overcome their past karmic life experiences while learning many great positive lessons.

When the time comes for you to transition out of your body, you have a life review with the True Sources' created resources (guardian angel, guides, master guides, etc.). It is important to understand that your life review includes reviewing everyone you have ever had contact with, whether it be positive or negative. You will feel the impact emotionally and energetically, firsthand, as each person experienced it by your words, deeds, and thoughts. This experience is not a punishment, but merely intended to help you grow and understand how you affect others. This is part of your karmic experience in order to become more enlightened.

I believe if everyone understood about the Akashic records' existence and their purpose, we would all think twice before we did or said anything. The saying, "What goes around, comes around" is very true, but a better way of expressing this same concept is, "Do unto others as you would have them do unto you." In those two well-known expressions lies great wisdom and power that we all need to pay attention to and follow. The world at this time is in chaos. In fact, when I look at the history of the world, it always seems to have been in chaos.

I would like to add a final thought: Now that you realize the impact we, as individuals and groups, have upon one another, it is never too late to change. While you cannot change the past, you can change the present and the future. Start now!

"Everything that has ever happened, is happening, and can happen is recorded in the Akashic Records. The existence of such energetic records has been known by people worldwide and is called by various names, including the 'Book of Life' in the Bible."

— Akemi G.

What role does ego play in our lives?

For me to answer this question, you must first understand that when you are born, everything is new and your life is a blank canvas. As time goes by, the veil of forgetfulness begins to descend upon you and you begin to miss your (telepathic) communications with your angels and guides. As you forget, you create another energetic vibration called the ego. You create the ego because you miss the telepathic communications with God, the True Source's created resources. At first, the ego is part of your support team, but as time goes by, it energetically begins to create a frequency vibration and energy of its own. The ego has one purpose: self-gratification. As it transitions into focusing solely on self-gratification, it begins to "Edge God Out," an accurate definition for ego as an acronym.

It is important to know that the ego can be your friend or your foe. For example, if you see someone excelling at something and you want to do well at it, your ego can spur you on to do so. On the other hand, if you ignore your ego, it will push your buttons to keep you under control, even if it is detrimental to you. The question then is: How do we handle the ego, and how do we know whether we are acting based upon ego or spiritual guidance/truth? If it is ego, it always has to justify its reasoning, even if it is flawed. For example, it might tell you, "Purchase that car. It will be a good car even though it's expensive. You're going to feel great and wonderful. Your friends will be jealous. You will figure out how to afford it." If it is God, the True Source's spiritual advice, then it will make a flat statement, "Buy the car." Remember God, the True Source knows exactly what your needs are and will supply all that is needed for you to obtain and maintain the car. This also applies to anything else you are receiving from God, the True Source. Think of it this way: You ask the question, "Is it raining?" If the answer is "Yes," that is spiritual guidance, or as I call it, God, the True Source's inner guidance. If it is ego, the answer might be, "There is a deluge of water going on outside; listen to the windows being pounded by the rain; look at the puddles." It'll be multiple reasons to prove it is raining.

The next question you have is most likely: How do I control and deal with my ego? Most people try to ignore it, but at times, the ego will not let go; it'll keep resurfacing in your thoughts on what appears to be an ongoing basis. That would be like me telling you, "Don't think about the yellow lemon; don't think about the sour taste it will cause in your mouth; don't think about how it will make your mouth moist." The best way to handle the ego is to say, "Thank you. I appreciate your help, and I will get back to you." Then remind yourself that you are a beautiful, perfect, aspect of God, the True Source, and that you encompass the energy, frequency, and vibration of God, the True Source. Realize that you are completely in charge of your life with all its challenges, so you can heal all facets of your life and bring about your heart's desire. God, the True Source is *pure unconditional love*, and that is *you*!

Why do some of the spiritual "tools" (practices) many of us have learned over the years no longer work or seem diminished in their ability to achieve the spiritual outcome we so desire?

God, the True Source, keeps raising the vibrations, energies, and levels of this planet and our universe so, as aspects of God, the True Source, we need to do the same to stay in touch. As these frequencies, vibrations, and levels increase, the old tools are no longer able to operate in that arena of energy. That does not mean that all of them are not working, but that their energies and vibrations are beginning to diminish as of this writing. This situation is being implemented because negativity in any way, shape, form, or manner is also increasing; therefore, we need to raise our vibrations and energy in order to rise above it. These new tools (practices), so to speak, are of a higher frequency and energy and accomplish much more than the old tools. Instead of using intermediary tools for assistance, we can now go directly to God, the True Source, or to God, the True

Source's created resources. Once you have learned to align yourself with God, the True Source, all things are possible just by asking with right action and correct exchange. Think of it this way, some of the other type of "tools" others have used are four-leaf clovers, candles, crystals, wands, or other talismans. These new energies and vibrations now enable you to go direct to God, the True Source, to achieve your desired outcome. It is like playing *Monopoly* and going directly to "Go" to collect $200.

Is it true that we live in a dual universe of light and dark, good and evil?

Yes, we do live in a dual universe because the universe basically has only two energies. They are love and anything that is not of love. There are only two basic vibrations: light and dark.

If you will take a moment to examine two words—love and fear—and enunciate each word slowly and separately, you will sense something different in the emotional level of each one. To understand this more fully, say "fear" seven times. Pay attention to the intonation in your voice, the feelings in your body, and your heart rate. After completing this exercise, take a deep breath and say "love" seven times. Once again, pay attention to the intonation in your voice, the feelings in your body, and your heart rate. Observe that you feel better, less intense, more at ease, and have a lightness about you when you say "love."

Have you ever walked into a dark room and felt a bit uneasy? Conversely, have you ever walked into a room full of light? Which felt freer and more comfortable to you? The answer is obvious. If you decided to stay in the dark room for a period of time, your senses would heighten and you might well become paranoid because you cannot see the unknown. I would venture to say that unless you were forced to stay in the dark room, you would do everything possible to exit it. However, staying in a room full of light will make you feel relaxed and at ease and make you want to remain for a period of time. This example demonstrates how light and dark energies also work.

A wide range of energies exist, from the highest energy, which is pure unadulterated unconditional love, to the lowest where fear exists. These energies are manifested by entities. Those entities are not of God, the True Source's light (love) but are of dark/negative entities. They go by different names, including biblical and other ones. The truth is that negative/dark entities do exist in the universe since there are all types of entities vibrating at different levels and energies. Those who choose to be in light and follow a positive belief system or a higher expression of energy are vibrating at a higher loving level, a level that, to some degree, is that of God, the True Source's energy of love. Love is the highest, purest vibration in the universe. Nothing negative can survive without some semblance of love. Love is the glue that holds everything together, animate and inanimate. Without love, your body, energy, and everything else would slowly begin to dissipate and cease to exist.

Negative entities are vibrating at a very low frequency, which is why they live in a low, negative energy, called fear, and are stuck in this lower vibration. They are stuck there because they are afraid that when they go to the higher vibrations, which are love, that they will be punished. What they do not realize is that they will learn whatever karmic lessons are needed for them to heal in order to take the next step, which is love and light.

These negative entities constantly need to be energized just like we in the higher vibrations require. Therefore, they look around for weak individuals so they can create fear and chaos in their lives; they then feed upon this chaos to reenergize themselves. When a soul lives in some kind of fear, its vibrations are lowered and it becomes a literal eating frenzy for the dark entities. Sometimes, the fear they create allows them temporarily to take over the soul's body. The key word here is *temporarily*! It is temporary because they cannot live in the higher vibrations of love without making a transition into that energy and bearing karmic consequences. What they are not aware of is that love is the glue that keeps them together. Even when they create fear in a person through doubt, insecurity, anxiety, paranoia, etc., that lower vibration is still mixed with love, though to a lesser degree. That small bit of love is what holds their form together.

Eventually, God, the True Source, catches up with the dark entities. They will then be given a choice to change their ways and understand the karmic lessons they have created. After they agree to this, a great positive transition takes place. If these negative entities choose not to embrace God, the True Source's energy of unconditional love, they are quarantined until such time when they are ready to make the change. They too, of course, have to understand karmically what they have created and go through the process of learning, healing, and working out their karma.

A person can only be taken advantage of by negative/dark entities through fear, anxiety, paranoia, and other negative emotions. These situations are only temporary. If you encounter a negative energy, it is important to remember you are stronger than it because you are vibrating at a higher level that is based in unconditional love. This higher energy level has been achieved simply by your knowledge and acceptance of your being an aspect of God, the True Source. Remember, God, the True Source, vibrates on only one frequency—an energy called unconditional love! By aligning yourself with the purity of that thought, nothing can ever cause harm to you. You are always more powerful than any negative/dark entities!

Why are there such negative souls who commit horrific crimes, and how do those souls become so negative?

Many reasons exist for these situations, but I will address the two key ones.

First, many times, although not every time, souls that incarnate into physical bodies become challenged in life by their karma and/or karmic debt and find it to be traumatic. However, the soul aligned itself with these challenges before it incarnated in order to heal its past lives' karma and karmic debt. Even so, the challenges can become so overwhelming sometimes that the person becomes angry or upset, which, consciously or not, invites in negative entities or negative energies. These negative entities or energies begin to take over the person's consciousness and ego in order to justify that person's anger and frustrations. As time goes by, these negative entities or energies force out the soul and begin to take over the person's body. That's when horrific crimes or an incident occur. One example of a person being taken over is the famous Green River killings in the State of Washington. Another is that of Jack the Ripper, who killed women and prostitutes in Victorian London.

The other key way that people become negative souls happens when a person transitions out of his or her body, and rather than returning to the bosom of God, the True Source, the soul is captured by negative entities and forced to do their bidding. This coercion is done through the use of negative energy and threats. The soul, being frightened and insecure, then goes into a fetus and is reborn with the intention to become a mass murderer, rapist, child molester, dictator, etc. to appease the negative entities.

You are probably now wondering, "Could this happen to me?" Now that you are aware of this situation, have read this book, and are aware of your vibrations and your connection with God, the True Source, all you have to do is ask that when the time comes for you to transition out of your body that you be protected with right action and correct exchange. Then when the time comes, you will go to the right place and be protected. Go towards the brilliant, beaming white light!

The next question you are probably asking is: Why does God, the True Source, permit this situation to happen? In the grand scheme of things, anything that is negative and not of love creates a karma that has to be answered. In human form, we can measure time in seconds, minutes, hours, days, months, and years. But in spiritual form, time does not exist as we know it on the earthly plane. Have you ever meditated and thought you had been meditating for two hours, but it turned out to be only ten minutes, or vice versa? That is an example of how time exists on the spiritual plane.

As I described earlier, when souls first began to leave the bosom of God, the True Source, to incarnate, some souls were jealous and wanted to be omnipotent. These negative entities are eventually captured by God, the True Source, and are appropriately taken care of. Sometimes, they are quarantined, but eventually, God, the True Source, visits them and gives them the opportunity to embrace unconditional love, which then transforms them. Other times, they are stripped of all their energies, vibrations, etc. and placed into a deep sleep. Eventually, God, the True Source, visits them and asks them to accept love, and when they do, they are rehabilitated, but are still responsible karmically.

How do I ensure that I transition from this life into the next properly?

I answered this question in the above question, but I feel it is important here to make sure you take the right path when it comes time for you to make your transition. Therefore, I want to provide you with a process for doing so. As with all the affirmations and exercises in this book, it is important that you do not take any short-cuts because that will only harm or block you. This is the protocol for you to make sure you transition correctly.

Begin with the Dream Heaven mantra and your 108 items.

As you perform the mantra, pay attention to what you are feeling, sensing, perceiving, and seeing. Describe these on the lines below.

_____

_____

_____

_____

_____

_____

_____

Ask for your perfect bubble of protection to surround you on all levels—the inner and outer planes and around your form.

Now, call upon God, the True Source, and God, the True Source's created resources. Request that when the time comes for you to transition, you will go directly to the bosom of God, the True Source, with love, joy, grace, ease, and ultimate protection at all levels, on the outer plane, inner plane, and in your form.

On the lines listed below, record any feelings, thoughts, sensations, and visions you have after you complete the exercise.

_____

_____

_____

_____

_____

_____

_____

Once you have completed this exercise, you can believe and trust that when the time comes, you will be protected, guided, and go to the correct place.

I wish to remind all of you at this time that your thoughts, focus, words, and intentions must be sincere and full of love. This will help you create the life you so desire and joyful, positive outcomes.

What are the benefits of meditation?

Meditation has numerous and wonderful benefits. Below are listed the most important ones in my opinion.

- Helps you focus on things that are important in your life.

- Reinforces your immune system. Statistics show that those who meditate have 50 percent less illnesses.

- Reduces stress, fear, loneliness, depression, and anxiety.

- Increases general wellbeing.

- Makes you less impulsive and more thoughtful in your decisions.

- Enhances self-esteem and self-acceptance.

- Improves resilience against pain and adversity.

- Increases optimism, relaxation, and awareness.

- Prevents emotional eating, smoking, and drug use.

- Improves your mood and emotional intelligence.

- Increases memory and recall.

- Enhances cognitive abilities and creativity.

- Helps with clarity on decision-making and problem-solving.

- Helps to process information more clearly.

- Helps to block distractions.

- Keeps your brain sharp.

- Helps to increase your immune system and energy levels.

- Regulates breathing and heart rate.

- Increases longevity by adding years to your life.

- Helps to decrease inflammatory disorders and asthma.

- Decreases the discomfort of premenstrual and meno-pausal syndromes.

- Helps to prevent arthritis, fibromyalgia, and other illnesses.

As of this writing, those souls I have had the joy and honor of spiritually coaching and who have meditated have seen many changes in their lives, including but not limited to looking younger, and having their intuition and knowingness go from nonexistent to expanding to levels they never imagined. Their manifestation abilities have also grown so that they have attracted prosperity, abundance, perfect health, joy, and happiness into their lives. The exciting part is that the more they meditate, the more all these benefits are expanding exponentially for them.

How does work, especially in the corporate world, affect our energy?

This question is a great opportunity for us to understand how vortices operate. In the corporate world, the collective thought of the founder and employees begins to create a swirling energy called a vortex. After a period of time, this vortex begins to take on an energy and an intelligence of its own. It then attracts those persons who are either vulnerable, desperate, or in sync with the energy created by that vortex. The vortex may be self-serving if the corporation and its founders are; in that case, it has only one desire and goal: to fulfill the initial purpose of the corporation and its founders. This vortex begins to expand and incorporate more of its ideals and continues to be more self-serving. Have you ever known people who constantly talk about the company they work for and are sincerely dedicated to that company, even at the expense of their own personal health and cost? That person is generally in the company's vortex. If a person working for a company does not fit within its vortex, perhaps because she disagrees with the corporation's precepts or with fellow employees, she will eventually be "surplused." (What a great name for being laid off or fired. That is how negative corporations and their vortexes change definitions and names to fulfill their purposes.)

Vortices can also operate in other organizations, such as within a family, religion, fraternal organization, small business, or any type of personal relationship. It is important to realize that these vortices control and manipulate those involved without those people ever being aware of it. The vortices, because of the founders and employees' energy, develop their own rules, regulations, ethics, behaviors, and expectations, whether realistic or not. The vortex is self-serving to itself, at all costs.

Many people who become entrepreneurs and are self-employed may not realize it is the vortex they were working for that created the need for them to break away and go beat their own drums. At some level, they knew they did not fit in and were better suited to be on their own. If you have found yourself locked into one of these vortices, then perhaps it is very necessary for you to make a decision: to be or not to be part of the vortex or any vortices. Through deep meditation with God, the True Source, you can also retain your identity, and at the same time, be able to coexist with the vortex, but not be of the vortex. This is very important. Remember that vortices can apply to all levels of your life—family, friends, church, clubs, etc. It is also best to understand that a vortex spinning clockwise pulls you into the energy of it and is negative. A vortex spinning counterclockwise pulls all negative energy and allows you the freedom of choice, including connecting or reconnecting with higher spirituality and the energy of God, the True Source.

Let's do an exercise now to help you decide what to do about the vortices you are experiencing.

Make a list of what you enjoy about the vortices I've described above.

_____

_____

_____

_____

Make a list of what you find confining or disagreeable about these vortices.

_____

_____

_____

_____

_____

_____

_____

Decide what steps you are going to take to make the vortex you are involved in palatable or to break away from it.

_____

_____

_____

_____

_____

_____

_____

In dealing with your vortices, you may find this affirmation helpful:

I call upon God, the True Source, God, Dream Heaven, God the True Source's created resources, and God, the True Source's miracle medium of love to guide me in a clear and concise manner, which I cannot misunderstand and is not of my ego, and to assist me in making a decision concerning the vortex of _____ on the outer and inner planes and in my form, with love, joy, grace, ease, harmony, peace, and protection. So be it!

Once you repeat the affirmation, it is best to relax. The answer to your situation will eventually come to you clearly and concisely.

Can you explain why men and women are so different and how they can best connect in a relationship?

Many books have been written about relationships. In fact, I plan to write a book about it from a spiritual perspective. Let me give a concise answer here to this huge topic.

Many relationships were preordained before incarnation. They may be for closure purposes, to heal some kind of karma or karmic debt, or to fulfill your life's plan. I have a wonderful client who asked for counseling while also desiring to learn about spirituality. We both later discovered that in a past life, I was her father and she was my daughter. I cannot describe the joy and happiness I felt at discovering her once again. Like me, she is very intuitive. She pointed out to me that most men need to be stroked and encouraged, and although they can be strong in their business lives, in their personal and family lives, they have a constant need to feel supported. My observations with many males have shown this to be true. While most males are unaware of this, they appreciate the stroking; however, they forget that the stroking needs to be reciprocal. Some men always need to be the center of attention. She also pointed out to me that although women can be judgmental and catty, they also have a need for compassion from one another. By observing other women, she could point out that most women can get along fairly well with each other, but the minute a male enters their conversation or lives, their relationships with other women can become tenuous, and they can even become angry or verbally combative. Furthermore, when men leave the company of women, things calm down and the women begin to feel compassion and spiritual love for one another.

Why does this situation occur? Part of the reason is because women spend so much time as caretakers to their children, mothers, fathers, husbands, and others that they relish the chance of being with other women who are not attention abusers and do not feel the weight of family obligations. This situation is comparable to a sorority or club of appreciation for one another where the women can all speak of their trials and tribulations, feel supported, have the same things in common, and feel free if only for a few hours.

Men, on the other hand, feel the weight of being a parent and, though it's becoming rarer now, the family's sole financial supporter. As little boys, men feel close to their mothers and seek to be supported and consoled by them. I have observed this as the case with my grandsons toward their mother and with other mothers and their sons. Unintentionally, this situation sets up a pattern where most men seek female support when they are in a crisis. Obviously, this is a learned condition that continues throughout a male's life. While this situation does not apply to all males, it applies to the vast majority of them.

All spirituality comes from the feminine side of us. Therefore, it was natural for women to bring their spirituality from God, the True Source, in order to create a perfectly balanced energy for all the inhabitants on this planet. The male energy was designated to take the creative feminine energy and ground it on this planet to create a marriage of the two so there would be spirituality coupled with third-dimensional energies to achieve this goal. The dimensional energy can be best described as a forceful energy to create what is needed at the time on this planet. I know what you are thinking; it has gone or is skewed. No argument there; however, I believe things will change in the not-too-distant future to bring us into oneness in harmony.

Now that both sexes have read this information, it is my fervent hope that they will learn to support each other equally and understand one another's needs in order to have a complete and whole relationship. This is a karmic lesson for both males and females.

You often talk about how men and women balance each other out or can be each other's soulmates, but you also talk about how God does not have a gender. How important is gender, and can the same balance be found in same-sex relationships that you describe between men and women? Are same-sex relationships equally valid to those between men and women?

If we look at LGBT relationships, each partner is in a relationship no matter what his or her choice of physical body is. The partners' energetic bodies, vibrations, and frequencies are the opposite of each other so that they are in harmony and balance with each other, no matter what sex they appear to be. That is the law of the universe. No matter what your apparent sexuality appears to be in human form, frequencies and vibration are always in harmony and perfect balance.

Why do some souls choose to have a gay (homosexual or lesbian) experience?

Many times, after a soul births out of its body (passes on), it realizes it may have a lot of unfinished karmic/debt that was not completed for some reason in that lifetime. It, therefore, decides to reincarnate as quickly as it can to complete the task. In doing so, it has not had enough time to heal and rehabilitate itself. Its only concern is to complete unfinished karmic debt from its previous lifetime. It then chooses the next body available to incarnate. This may occur weeks or months before the fetus is incarnated or during or shortly after the fetus is incarnated. By doing so, it may inhabit a body that is not the same sex as it was in the past life. For example, it may have been male in its recent past life but now inhabit a female body. In its rush to incarnate, it has not considered being the same sex it was in a past life. Therefore, it takes on the same energy, frequency, and vibration of the sex it was in the past lifetime. One reason it may not have considered that fact is because in our soul embodiment, we are surrounded with love and our energy is androgynous. However, in its soul consciousness, even though its physical body is female, it still feels male. It then meets another soul that was female in a past life and now inhabits a body that is male. Even though the body is male, the soul still feels female. This example applies to why certain souls become lesbians or homosexuals. By the Law of Attraction, each soul is attracted to another by similar pheromones. If we take a moment to realize that it makes no difference what our body is or what our soul urges are, you can understand why different types of relationships occur. There are other karmic reasons why a soul chooses to be lesbian or homosexual, but the most overwhelming reason is what I have described above.

Whether you agree or disagree with the life paths these souls have chosen, it is important for each of us to recognize they have chosen very difficult life paths due to our misguided religious belief systems. We must stop to remember that all of us are an aspect of God, the True Source, and that each one of us is growing and evolving in the way we have chosen. I believe it is incumbent for each one of us to honor the life paths these beautiful souls have chosen to experience in order to grow, experience life, and evolve. Honor them, and remember they are as much a part of you as you are of them because your pure essence, like all others', is that of God, the True Source.

Why does emotional bondage/cords occur?

The best way to describe how emotional bondage occurs is to look at the belief systems developed in early life that are inspired by friends or family members who fill a child with fear, doubt, anxiety, and a sense of limitation. These thoughts are first observed by the conscious mind, then the subconscious, and they finally are absorbed into our cellular structure. It is important to realize that when I talk of your cellular structure, it includes every part of your beingness as well as every organ that stores energy and memory; as a result, this absorption of negative thoughts can affect you physically, mentally, and emotionally. We, intentionally or unintentionally, become subservient to these feelings, and they, in turn, create prisons in our lives and relationships. As I have pointed out before, the unconscious mind only thinks in positive and negative, not in gray areas; it is not logical or thoughtful. Therefore, the cellular structure only behaves and responds to whatever is placed into it. While thoughts of joy and youthfulness might benefit you, negative thoughts can create physical or mental limitations, illness, and emotional bondage.

Emotional bondage becomes a set of rules for our lives that limit us to the extent that we believe in them. These thoughts and emotions then have the power to control and manipulate our lives in negative ways; this situation is contrary to God, the True Source's desire for us to have lives that will bring us happiness at all levels. Stop for a minute and think how powerful your thoughts and emotions are. As I explained earlier, you only need to change your thoughts three degrees, from -1 to 0 to +1. That's a very small shift in thought. You can do this by repeating a positive affirmation at least once a day for a minimum of thirty days so it becomes embedded in your conscious, subconscious, and cellular structure. Then the emotional bondage will be released.

I have worked with many souls and found that repeating a positive affirmation anywhere from 30 to 120 days works 99.9 percent of the time. The other 0.1 percent have to do it a little bit longer. The object of this is exercise is to realize that by changing your thoughts, you can change your life; it is really that simple. Remember, you are your thoughts, and thoughts become things, and things become alive and active in your life. Thoughts can either enhance or hinder your life—it's your choice!

To release yourself from emotional bondage, first make a list of the emotions that keep you in bondage.

_____

_____

_____

_____

_____

_____

Now, you may either use this affirmation or create your own. The important thing to remember is to repeat it for each individual limitation of bondage you have, one at a time for a minimum of thirty days until you are no longer bound physically, mentally, and emotionally by it.

I call upon God, the True Source, God, God the True Source's created resources, and God, the True Source's miracle medium of love to be healed and freed of my emotional bondage of

_____ now with love, grace, harmony, balance, ease, and perfection on the outer and inner planes and in my form. So be it!

If you so desire, create your own affirmation. Just be sure to follow the timeframe.

At this point, it is also important for you to realize that everything that occurs in your life is a gift, even though it may seem like a momentous roadblock. It is there for each one of us to look at, examine, and overcome, for it may be karma or a karmic debt. Once overcome, it is gone forever, but if not acted upon, it will keep you in chains.

It is interesting how many people come up with excuses for why they cannot do something when the truth is they just enjoy being in the victim mode. I once again remind you that every action causes a reaction. You can choose positivity or negativity. Just remember, there is always a payoff. Everything you do always has a payoff. As for me, I choose a payoff of positivity, joy, happiness, abundance, prosperity, and perfect health. What do you choose?

Each morning when you wake up, think about how wonderful it is to be alive. Then ask yourself what you desire to create in this day of your life. Ask God, the True Source, that you fulfill your mission and goal for that day. At the end of the day, ask to know whether you have done your mission and goal, and if not, how you could have achieved it. Ask for assistance to fulfill your mission and goal each and every day. In complying with this, you are doing the work of the Divine, and by the laws of karma and the universe, it will come back to you more than ten thousand fold. Do it out of love and joy, not out of expectation or need. If you will promise yourself to do this every day, you will see love, joy, and thankfulness. In turn, you will be filled with unconditional love and everything in your life will support you in bringing about unconditional love beyond what you could ever conceive.

Is it possible to heal your body?

The answer is unequivocally yes. However, personal self-healing requires a certain protocol, beginning with the necessity for you to believe that you are now going to be healed! This means that not in the future, but at this moment you must believe it. If your belief is not strong enough, then there is a block about worthiness. All that is necessary is for you to repeat the sequence described below over and over again, positively believing that you will be healed and it will be achieved.

To assist you in healing, it is important for you to realize that God, the True Source, loves you unconditionally and desires for you to be perfect in every way. As you embrace this belief, you are 90 percent underway to being perfectly healed. The other 10 percent is stepping out of your emotional doubt, negative self-worth or self-esteem, guilt, anxiety, impatience, and frustrations. Remember the old saying, "God doesn't make any junk." I would like to remind you that you are a perfect aspect of God, the True Source.

It is also necessary for you to surround yourself only with positive people. If you have any naysayers in your life, do not discuss with them that you are in the process of healing yourself. The naysayers are doubters, and they will, intentionally or unintentionally, fail to support you, and worse, could make you doubt yourself and lose your belief that you can heal. Again, surround yourself only with positive people.

Here is the five-step protocol I would suggest for healing yourself:

1. Ask God, the True Source, to surround you with the perfect bubble of protection at all levels, on the outer and inner planes and in your form.

2. Repeat the Dream Heaven mantra 108 times.

3. Ask God, the True Source, for the perfect healing of your body, mind, soul, spirit, emotions, psyche, ability to love, and every cell within and without on the outer plane, inner plane, and in your form. It is important that after reciting this affirmation, you take a few minutes to embrace this energy. You will feel some type of sensation in your body, such as tingling, warmth, cold, buzzing, or lightheadedness. After embracing the energy, repeat nine times: "I bless and release this _____ (describe in detail) with love. So be it."

4. The next step is to ask God, the True Source, to fill you with God, the True Source's unconditional love at the deepest cellular level, at the outer and inner planes, and in your form.

5. Next, relax and meditate for at least fifteen minutes. If your mind begins to wander or doubt, repeat the word "cancel" three times and affirm you are now healed. If your thoughts continue to wander, inhale "dream" and exhale "heaven." The reason it is necessary for you to say, "Cancel" three times is that there is no such thing as a vacuum in the universe, and by the Law of Manifestation, all thoughts must come to fruition. By repeating "cancel" and replacing it with a new positive thought, you prevent the previous negative thought from being manifested in your life.

6. Finally, repeat three times, "I give thanks. I give thanks. I give thanks. Thank you. Thank you. Thank you. So be it!"

Congratulations! You are now well on the way to being perfectly healed, or perhaps you are already healed.

I can personally attest that this protocol has worked well for me and many other souls I have shared it with.

CHAPTER 16

IMPORTANT AFFIRMATIONS TO ENHANCE YOUR LIFE

"I am in the process of becoming the best version of myself."

— **Unknown**

Here are some important affirmations that will assist you in your life. Each one has a specific vibration, energy, and frequency to achieve its goal.

These affirmations should be said every day, and whenever you feel the urge to do so, more than once a day. If you are feeling the need to say one or more of them during the day, that is because your soul is telling you that they are needed in your life at that moment. There may be some reason for this that you're not aware of, but it will make sense to you later, and then you will be happy that you said them.

THE PERFECT BUBBLE OF PROTECTION

I call upon God, the True Source, Dream Heaven, God, the True Source's created resources, and God, the True Source's miracle medium of love to surround me with a bubble of protection in and around and about me at all levels, on the outer plane, inner plane, and in my form.

The definition of God, the True Source's created resources are your guides, master guides, guardian angel(s), angels, archangels, etc. The definition of the outer plane is everything around you in human form; the inner plane is the spiritual plane, and your form is your body. The two most powerful words in the universe are "I AM." These two words affirm that you exist and, simultaneously, are one with God, the True Source, and God, the True Source, is one with you, and in a sense, you are the same, meaning an aspect of God, the True Source. "Dream Heaven" are the second two most powerful words in the universe; what they do is raise your vibrations and consciousness to connect with God, the True Source, at the highest level you are capable of achieving. This affirmation protects you against all kinds of harm. It also means that you will know after you have invoked this affirmation of protection whether you are in any danger and how to prevent that from occurring.

HEALING: NOT BEING IN THE NEGATIVE ENERGY OF EARTH

I call upon God, the True Source, Dream Heaven, God, the True Source's created resources, and God, the True Source's miracle medium of love that I be of this planet, but not of the negative emotion of this planet, at all levels, on the outer plane, inner plane, and in my form for multi-dimensional healing.

I call upon God, the True Source, Dream Heaven, God, the True Source's created resources, and God, the True Source's miracle medium of love to send whole and complete healing of body, mind, soul, spirit, love, emotion, psyche, and every cell within and without on all levels on the outer plane, inner plane, and in their form to heal my _____.

At the end, state the person's name. You must recite this affirmation individually for each person. It is also necessary for you to know that the person you are sending healing to has a right to accept or reject the healing. The beautiful part about this affirmation is when someone is ready to receive it, it will enter into his or her multi-dimensional bodies and beingness. I also strongly suggest that you do not tell the person you are saying this affirmation until after he or she is healed. I have run across some people who either don't believe it or don't feel they are worthy of being healed, and thus, they may block it. It is also important to know that if it is someone's time to "birth out" of his or her body, the transition will be made easier.

TRANSFORMATIONAL CELLULAR LOVE ENERGY

I call upon God, the True Source, Dream Heaven, and God, the True Source's created resources to fill me with God, the True Source's unconditional love at the deepest cellular level in my multi-dimensional bodies at all levels, on the outer plane, inner plane, and in my form.

The purpose of this affirmation is to achieve inner peace and healing on the physical, mental, and emotional bodies, and at all levels.

ANTI-AGING AFFIRMATION

I call upon God, the True Source, Dream Heaven, and God, the True Source's created resources that I now be the perfect chronological and biological age of_____ at all levels, on the outer plane, inner plane, and in my form. (Insert your desired age).

Power Affirmations Before Sleep

To achieve healing and inner peace in your life, I suggest that just before you go to sleep, you use the following two affirmations:

1. Look into the mirror and say, *I love you*, _____ (saying your name) three times with great emotion.

2. Follow this up with saying three times with great emotion: *I am unlimited!*

These two powerful affirmations will change your life in a positive way. It is important that you say them each and every night for the rest of your days to keep the energy flowing. The first affirmation, saying that you love yourself, achieves many things. Let me enumerate on a few of them. It teaches you to love yourself, it tells your total being that you love yourself just as you are, and it allows you to heal physically, mentally, energetically, and emotionally. It brings into your life all things that you love, including but not limited to joy, happiness, prosperity, healing, abundance, relationships, and many more. The second affirmation makes you feel at your very core that you can achieve anything and everything you so desire in life; it is only limited by your thoughts, while it is unlimited because what your soul desires is what is best for you.

THE SPIRITUAL FORMULA FOR RELEASING PENT UP EMOTIONS, NEGATIVE ENERGY, ANXIETY, FRUSTRATIONS, ETC.

This simple exercise helps to release all negative pent-up emotions, negative energy, anxiety, frustrations, etc. It is especially helpful for those who are empaths!

As I have explained in previous chapters, it is important to put up your bubble of protection. Once you have completed this, it is highly advisable that you repeat the Dream Heaven mantra 108 times. I know when a person is anxiety-ridden that it is hard to follow this protocol; however, you will be amazed by how well it works.

Once you have completed the protocol (placed the perfect bubble of protection around you and completed repeating the Dream Heaven mantra 108 times), you are now prepared to release successfully all the stressful energies I mentioned in the first paragraph.

Now that you have found a quiet place, speak the following affirmation: *I release with love [state what you are desiring to release] now with love, joy, grace, harmony, balance, ease, and protection on the outer plane, inner plane, and in my form.* Just a reminder, the outer plane is everything around you, the inner plane is the spiritual plane, and your form is your body. Repeat this affirmation 108 times until you feel a release of energy. Without doubt, if you repeat this affirmation as often as necessary, you will achieve great success. The more you do so, the sooner it will happen.

AFFIRMATION TO CLEAR NEGATIVE ENERGIES WHEN THIS ENERGY BREAKS THROUGH YOUR "BUBBLE OF PROTECTION"

I call upon God, the True Source, Dream Heaven, God, the True Source's Created Resources, and God, the True Source's Miracle Medium of Love, that all negative entities, negative energies, negative ETs, negativity, and negative implants now be cleared, and Dream Heaven at all levels, on the outer plane, inner plane, and in their form, and in my form be established. And it is so, so be it. I give thanks. I give thanks. I give thanks.

NOTE: My clients tell me this last affirmation and the "Bubble of Protection" are two of the most commonly used and effective ones to practice daily. I have more than one hundred additional affirmations and manifestations that I coach and teach, but there is not enough space in this book to include them all here. To learn more about them, I encourage you to schedule your complimentary consultation or healing with me by texting your name and time zone to me at (253) 222-1096.

CHAPTER 17

WORDS AND THOUGHTS
OF WISDOM

"Stay away from negative people. They have a problem for every solution."
— **Albert Einstein**

The past predicts the present and the present predicts the future. You probably understand part of what this sentence means. If you live in the past, challenges, blocks, fears, etc. will own you and control you well into the future. In essence, when you are first born, it is as if your life is a blank canvas and you are the artist who will create your life. You chose life to experience love, joy, happiness, karmic challenges, and so on. You chose these to learn and grow while working to achieve your mission and goal. What a *beautiful* and *herculean life* you have created for yourself, knowing full well that you are the *master of your life*. What does that mean? It means you have the innate ability to change and create any and all experiences in your life.

Everything you have learned from the time of your first breath and to this very moment has been recorded not only in the Akashic

Records (your book of life) but also in your memory banks and your body's cellular structure. Take a few minutes to contemplate your life and look at your blocks, fears, doubts, insecurities, lack of self-worth, lack of self-esteem, lack of self-love, and also all the positive, wonderful, loving things you have created. If any of the challenges I have described control your life, realize those obstacles were created from the *Past*, exist in the *Present*, and if not changed, will continue to hinder you in the *Future*.

You need to take three steps in order to change anything currently hindering your life:

Step One: Realize that this obstacle in your life is nothing but a challenge, and you created it to grow and empower yourself so that it may never occur again. Meditate on it so that you have a clear and concise understanding of it.

Step Two: It is important to know that all obstacles are gifts—yes, gifts—that you created in your life to empower you. Then ask, God, the True Source, to assist you in releasing this obstacle.

Step Three: Repeat this affirmation a minimum of thirty-six times per day: *I Bless and Release this (fear, block, or whatever it may be but describe it in detail) with love for my soul and higher self. So Be It!* Then when you have finished doing it thirty-six times, end with, *I give thanks. I give thanks. I give thanks. Thank you! Thank you! Thank you!* Repeat this until you feel a shift of energy and realize it is no longer part of your life. You will feel lighter and clearer then, knowing full well it is healed and over and done with. Do not give up, no matter how long it may take. You may repeat this affirmation in groups of thirty-six as many times a day as you feel you need to; your soul is now guiding you in the healing process. The more frequently you do this, the quicker the healing will be.

CHAPTER 18

THOUGHTS TO LIVE BY

"You are the sky. Everything else—it's just the weather."

— Pema Chodron

In your journey called life, I would like to share the following wisdom with you:

- Each disappointment is but a challenge to grow and learn.

- We learn not only from our successes but also from our failures. Learn well!

- When you feel you have missed an opportunity and the door seems to close, another door of opportunity always opens.

- Never live in the past for it serves no purpose except to place you in a prison of anger and block the unlimited future.

- Never hold onto anger because in time it will affect your physical body and your mental health.

- Always remember to forgive yourself for any mistakes you have made and forgive others for their mistakes. The purpose of doing this is to free yourself of anxiety and emotional pain so you can always move forward.

- Always strive to be a student to learn and never think you know everything.

- Become mindful and listen before you speak so that your words and thoughts are of great wisdom.

- There are only two energies on this planet: Love and anything that is not of love. Become Love!

- One of my favorite quotes from Henry Ford, the great automobile manufacturer, is: "Whether you think you can or you think you can't, you're right!"

- Remember, you are unlimited and only limited by your fears, thoughts, insecurities, and doubts. Become unlimited!

- Everyone who comes into your life is your teacher and you are the student; conversely, you are their teacher and they are your student.

- Fear is an illusion created by the unknown.

- Knowledge is power.

- Wisdom is strength.

Two quotes I received in meditations I would like to share with you.

"What the mind can conceive, the body will believe."

"The past is but an experience. The present is but a moment. The future is but a thought."

Please think about those quotes because I believe you will obtain much wisdom from them.

I leave you with this thought a dear friend and student of mine, Howard Grosse, received from Spirit and shared with me:

"There is no yesterday, there is no tomorrow; there is only the now forever."

And finally one of my favorite Albert Einstein quotes is:

"Everything is energy and that's all there is to it. Match the frequency of the reality you want and you cannot help but get that reality. It can be no other way. This is not philosophy. This is physics."

A FINAL NOTE

EXPERIENCING LOVE, JOY, AND HAPPINESS

"Set out each day believing in your dreams. Know without a doubt that you were made for amazing things."

— Josh Hinds

I could not begin to conclude this book without discussing Lady Gaia, which is also known as Mother Earth. In my meditations and conversations with Mother Earth, she said that she is hurting because the human race has forgotten her as a living, breathing entity. She works in concert with the nature spirits to provide for us, and yet very few appreciate what is given and sacrificed for us.

I have contemplated the beautiful balance on this planet that is now becoming skewed. Stop for a moment and think how without the bees, we would have no honey; there would be no cross-pollination; therefore, it would interfere with food production. Without the rain, we could not exist nor flourish because there would be no food. Without the trees and grass inhaling carbon dioxide and exhaling oxygen, we could not breathe. Without Mother Earth's minerals and oils, we could not build nor have transportation as we know it now. Without the sun, not only would things not grow, but we would not be producing vitamin D and other types of nutrients that are necessary for us. If we look at our bodies, we realize Mother Earth produces certain minerals that we need to support our metabolism and metabolic systems. The animals sacrifice themselves, sometimes unwillingly, to feed us while the sun, moon, and weather nurture us.

If we think about such a delicate balance on this planet, and the gift of procreation and how it takes place in the female and male, it is totally mind-boggling, at least for me, and I hope you feel the same way. I could elaborate even more, but I feel at this time you can now comprehend what I am saying. The nature spirits told me that they are unhappy with the way the inhabitants of this planet are spraying poisons, destroying vegetation to build huge buildings and roads that pollute not only Mother Earth but all the aspects of the animal, mineral, and vegetable kingdoms. Yes, they are kingdoms in the largest sense of the word that we helped design eons ago to support each one of us individually and jointly in body, mind, soul, spirit, and much more. I do not look upon myself as an environmentalist, but rather as a spiritual soul, awakening all who will listen and read what I have to say in order to awaken and preserve the sanctity of all types of life that exists in order to help change our consciousness to reconnect with God, the True Source.

Thank you for taking this journey with me. You've now finished this book, but more importantly, you've begun an exciting new journey toward increased enlightenment. Now that you've made it this far, there is no turning back. You will now begin to observe many positive empowering changes in your life much to your delight. You will become a beacon of change, not only for yourself, but for your family, relatives, friends, coworkers, and the place where you work. You have just begun a powerful journey of enlightenment, love, joy, prosperity, abundance, and perfectly enduring health that will continue for the rest of your life.

Take a moment to reflect upon that last sentence. Then make a list below of the changes you have discovered in a positive way about your life from reading this book and doing the exercises.

EXERCISE

List the changes that you now sense and feel in your life.

_____

_____

_____

_____

Record the changes in your relationships:

Family:

_____

_____

_____

_____

Friends:

_____

_____

_____

_____

Work:

_____

_____

_____

_____

Mental changes:

_____

_____

_____

_____

Emotional changes:

_____

_____

_____

_____

Physical changes:

_____

_____

_____

_____

Psychological changes:

_____

_____

_____

_____

Your feelings about yourself:

_____

_____

_____

_____

Your feelings about your life:

_____

_____

_____

_____

Observe and record how strangers and others respond to you:

_____

_____

_____

_____

You have donned the warrior suit to make these changes, and you will no longer be stuck in the status quo. You have challenged yourself, your belief system, and society to make these positive changes. You've grown emotionally, mentally, energetically, and spiritually at many different levels as you've achieved positive alignment with God, the True Source. By achieving this great feat, you have come to realize you are an aspect of God, the True Source, and therefore, now your communications are becoming clearer and clearer, moment by moment, and day by day. Blessings upon you. You are now aware of your connection to the Divine!

But you need to be more than just aware. While it's great that you sense the changes in yourself and your life, you also need to be a positive source for change for the rest of the universe, so you have one more consideration. Ask yourself, "How can I apply all of the twelve laws plus everything else I have learned in this book to my work life, family life, and social life?" You see, our life is a matter of choices, but ultimately, we have two types of choices; the first choice we usually make out of desperation and perceived necessity, but the second choice is the one that is best for our higher selves, which brings about the fulfillment of our soul and heart's desire.

Tell yourself now, "From this point on, I am going to make decisions based not only on what is best for my higher self, but also what is best for my family, friends, relatives, work, and all others I am involved with. In truth, what is best for your higher self is God, the True Source's divine unconditional love. That love allows each of us to have a life filled with harmony, joy, happiness, prosperity, abundance, and perfect health, thus creating a circle of energy around the earthly sphere that brings about all that is perfect for ourselves, our families, our careers, our friends, and our lives. It all starts with each one of us individually, and then it merges into ever converging and concentric circles, creating a frequency and energy that attracts to us everything we desire in a state of harmony and balance.

At a macro level, God, the True Source, is the creator of all, and at a micro level, we are the creators of our lives. In order for this abundant and joyous existence to be achieved, we have to be in harmony and balance not only with God, the True Source, but also with our individual selves (including with our soul and oversoul), our missions and goals, Mother Earth, and all those around us. While this process may seem monumental to some, to others it represents the ebb and flow of life, manifesting what is best for all involved, including ourselves.

EXERCISE

Make a list of how you can apply God's Twelve Transformational Laws to your everyday life.

1. The Law of Love

_____

_____

2. The Law of One

_____

_____

3. The Law of Manifestation

_____

_____

4. The Law of Karma

_____

_____

5. The Law of Enlightenment

_____

_____

6. The Law of Non-Judgment

_____

_____

7. The Law of Perfect Health

_____

_____

8. The Law of Prosperity

_____

_____

9. The Law of Gratitude

_____

_____

10. The Law of Surrender

_____

_____

11. The Law of Perfection

_____

_____

12. The Law of Compassionate Understanding and Forgiveness

_____

_____

Make a list of how you can apply God's Twelve Transformational Laws to your everyday life.

1. The Law of Love

_____

_____

2. The Law of One

_____

_____

3. The Law of Manifestation

_____

_____

4. The Law of Karma

_____

_____

5. The Law of Enlightenment

_____

_____

6. The Law of Non-Judgment

_____

_____

7. The Law of Perfect Health

_____

_____

8. The Law of Prosperity

_____

_____

9. The Law of Gratitude

_____

_____

10. The Law of Surrender

_____

_____

11. The Law of Perfection

_____

_____

12. The Law of Compassionate Understanding and Forgiveness

_____

_____

Make a list of how you can apply God's Twelve Transformational Laws to your everyday life.

1. The Law of Love

_____

_____

2. The Law of One

_____

_____

3. The Law of Manifestation

_____

_____

4. The Law of Karma

_____

_____

5. The Law of Enlightenment

_____

_____

6. The Law of Non-Judgment

_____

_____

7. The Law of Perfect Health

_____

_____

8. The Law of Prosperity

_____

_____

9. The Law of Gratitude

_____

_____

10. The Law of Surrender

_____

_____

11. The Law of Perfection

_____

_____

12. The Law of Compassionate Understanding and Forgiveness

_____

_____

Review these notes every thirty days to see how your efforts are positively affecting and changing your life, and make any adjustments necessary. At the end of each thirty-day period, make a little note of the changes you have experienced, and then the next month, track your progress to see how much more positive magic has occurred in your life!

*"The world as we have created it is a process of our thinking.
It cannot be changed without changing our thinking."*

— Albert Einstein

Your journey is just beginning. I promise you much positive magic yet to come. Enjoy the journey!

THE TWELVE
MANIFESTATION PROTOCOLS

YOUR PERSONAL PATH
TO CREATING THE LIFE
OF YOUR DREAMS

"What You Think, You Create. What You Create, You Experience."

— **Dr. Michael Gross/T.S.**

I would like to share how I began teaching the manifestation protocols. In the fall of 2019, The True Source came to me and said I was to teach manifestation again. I put the class together and started teaching in March 2020. Little did I know how seriously the coronavirus would affect humankind. We are all aware of how businesses closed down and masks were mandated, causing confusion and economic fear. At that time, the class was designed to be eight sessions, which we completed successfully.

In 2021, The True Source asked me again to teach the class. This time, I was to make it twelve sessions long, with each session being ninety minutes. I began to have visions of me teaching it in the ancient mystery schools, which had existed several thousand years before. I was also told to go into deeper depth. Originally, more than twenty-five souls started the class. In the beginning, they bemoaned that it was an hour and a half for each session as well as the course being twelve weeks long. By the time the course came to an end, they were amazed by how fast it went. The breakthroughs were phenomenal, and I can only thank The True Source for guiding me and helping all those souls to manifest their "perfect" lives. The reason for the manifestation protocols was to share with everybody that each one of us is the solution and can make a difference in this chaotic world. For you to achieve that difference, it is necessary for you to manifest your spiritual missions and goals!

Every soul has missions and goals. For example, if you are a parent, your vocations, relationships, and children are your spiritual missions. Through our missions and goals, we will change the energy and influence the planet's inhabitants. To reiterate, part of my mission and goal is to awaken 1 percent of the planet's population to change the mass consciousness so people will realize they can now connect with The True Source. Once 1 percent of people come to that realization, it becomes a vibration and energy that will awaken others from their deep sleep to realize they also have similar missions and goals, involving their families, vocations, spiritual missions, etc.

Once you have, figuratively, opened the door, I believe it is important for you to understand the mechanics of how manifestation works. As is evident, everything on this planet is made up of energy. Our very being, in essence, consists of intelligent energy. This energy consists of atoms, particles, molecules, subatomic structure electrons, etc. I call it "the soup mix" energy. I believe the best way to explain this energy is to look at a piece of wood. It appears solid. Scientists will tell you it is a certain number of atoms, particles, and electrons, and the rest of the energy soup mix is vibrating with a certain frequency and energy to create a solid piece of wood. If the energy were moving too fast, the piece of wood would not be created and "the soup mix" would literally disappear. If the energy were moving too slow, the "soup mix" particles could not be attracted to each other and therefore could not form.

Perhaps the easiest example to illustrate is to look at an ice cube. The energy of "soup mix" is moving very slowly and appears solid. That is because the freezing energy in the refrigerator slows down the atoms, etc. When you remove the ice cube and place it in a pot with the atoms, etc., the atoms begin moving a little more quickly because they are not slowed down by the cold. Speeding up the vibrations by adding heat, the atoms, etc., begins to move everything more quickly, and then the ice cube transforms from a solid to a liquid. As you add more energy, the energy "soup mix" begins to vibrate, move more quickly, and turn into steam. As more energy is added (more heat), the steam begins to rise and disappear before your eyes. That is because the atoms, particles, etc. are no longer attracted to each other. However, when you place your hand above the pot, your hand will collect water droplets. The reason is your hand over the pot is slowing down the vibrations by blocking the energy from continuing to go faster. Eventually, the water droplets on your palm will fall back into the pot. As you reduce the energy by shutting off the heat, the steam will become liquid, and by reducing the energy again, the energy "soup mix" will become a liquid. By further slowing down the energy and placing it in a freezer, the liquid becomes a solid. In other words, you have control of the energy using the various methods I described above.

Manifestation is best known as creation. Have you ever heard someone say, "You are very creative"? A strong correlation exists between manifestation and creation. In fact, they are the same. They are how you begin to create your life and all your experiences. They are the start of how you manifest your life and all aspects of your life.

Everything has a frequency, energy, vibration, and sound. Every word/thought has a frequency, energy, and vibration. Therefore, one of the best ways to manifest is to realize your thoughts and words create the vibration, energy, frequency, and sound to bring forth what you are thinking about into your reality. Henceforth, "What you think, You Create. What You Create, You Experience! T.S." It is important for each of us to remember we are creating our reality, our life each and every moment of our existence, or what we would call on a 24/7 basis.

Your thoughts and words consist of a mental image as well as an energetic image of whatever you desire to create in your life. The energy you use to create your life is unlimited and not based on distance. Remember, all energy is neutral. How you direct your thoughts and the concentrated energy in them achieves the final outcome. Time and distance do not make a difference. I believe the best way to think about it is to imagine you are talking on a cell phone. When you use your cell phone, it sends out a signal no matter where you are or what conditions you are experiencing. The signal reaches the person at the other end. Using this analogy, manifestation protocols and the energy needed for them have no distance limitations. Wherever you are, whatever you desire, you will manifest. In fact, you are manifesting everything in your life 24/7. I'm sure you have never thought about it. There are many, many methods of manifesting. However, all the other methods were created by people who doubted they could create anything without repetition. They came up with the idea to create vision boards. It is time for you to realize that nothing stands in your way of creating whatever you so desire in your life except you. Remember, "YOU ARE UNLIMITED!"™

Listed below are the Twelve Protocols for Manifestation with a brief explanation for each. An exercise follows each one so you can practice the protocol.

1. **The Belief Syndrome:** Whatever you believe you will manifest into your life, and it is important to remember that the subconscious mind does not differentiate between positive or negative. The Soul, however, does differentiate and will guide you to listen to the thoughts of your soul. It is important at this point that you begin with a clean slate to change your challenging belief system. That means letting go of anything that is limiting. You're probably wondering how you let go. The answer is simple! Just focus your thoughts and energy on the positive things you desire to manifest into your life. Below make a list of your limiting beliefs.

    _____

    _____

    _____

    _____

2. **Self-Worth:** You need to examine your feelings about yourself to realize the only inhibitor to creating your life of joy and happiness is failing to truly understand that you are worthy. Believing in our self-worth takes a great deal of introspection, for we, as humans, are great at lying to ourselves. When you understand the excuses that you make up about being unworthy, you are able to remove

the negative emotions around self-worth. Once that is accomplished, anything and everything is possible. Describe your feelings about your self worth in the lines below.

_____

_____

_____

_____

3. **Your Life Story:** The shadows of your past create the blocks in your current life and your future life. You may or may not be aware that you are living in the fears, doubts, and insecurities of your past. By now, you understand you are blocking your unlimited future. An old cliché says, "Thoughts are things." What it is saying is you are creating your beliefs by the experience of your limited past. It is best to know that your past was merely a series of experiences designed for you to learn what works and does not work for you. List below your limiting life stories and realize from those emotions and blocks how you have grown. Then create whatever you so desire.

_____

_____

_____

_____

_____

4. **Clearing Negative Thoughts:** Ninety-four percent of our thinking comes from the subconscious mind while 6 percent comes from the conscious mind. Your mind is a computer, and the computer's memory is your subconscious

mind. It contains all your experiences, both negative and positive. The subconscious mind come forth either affirming, negating, or blocking your experiences. As humans, we are always comparing the past with the present. Here's the example I use: If I were to say to you, "Let's have a hot fudge sundae," you would immediately go back to the last time you had one. If it were pleasant, you would immediately respond, "Let's do it." But if I said, "Let's have a hot fudge sundae with sauerkraut and ghost peppers," your response would be obvious. This begs the question: How do you eliminate and change your negative thoughts? Previously in this book, I gave you a phrase to use that I will share with you again. When a negative thought occurs, it's important to say "5, 4, 3, 2, 1, cancel, cancel, cancel," and replace it with a positive thought. Saying this phrase removes the thought from the upper hemispheres of your brain so it goes to the amygdala. This immediately breaks the energy of the thought and blocks it from becoming a reality. The reason you need to do this is there is no such thing as a vacuum in the universe, meaning every thought will eventually come into reality. If you say cancel, cancel, cancel and do not replace it with the new thought, then what happens is the old thought comes back into your reality. List below times when you have to use this exercise.

_____

_____

_____

_____

5. **Concentration:** The intensity of your focus on what you are manifesting adds rocket fuel to your thought of manifestation. The key at this point is to make sure you're not distracted. Become one with your manifestation and feel it as if it has already occurred without any doubt. The best way to achieve this focus is to imagine with deep concentration that it is already here and you are now experiencing it. For example, remember when you wanted something as a young child and you pretended that it was already part of your life? Use this or any other example to create those feelings. List below the various ways you can create these feelings.

_____

_____

_____

_____

6. **Vibrations:** Emotions are literally energies felt, either positive or negative, that you use to create your positive manifestation. The positive excitement in your emotions is what will speed up your manifestation, and the negative doubt in your emotions will either slow down or eliminate the manifestation from occurring. List below the emotions you need to create the excitement of your manifestation.

_____

_____

_____

_____

7.   **Frequencies:** A frequency is the rate at which you think positively with great excitement and positivity. It is best explained by saying "Like attracts like." Emotion placed into that thought that you are creating will accelerate everything you desire to manifest. This is best explained by thinking about the excitement you feel when your heart beats faster, your skin gets flushed, and you feel your warmth and excitement and a tingling in your body. List below some of those feelings. An example of this might be how you feel about buying your first car or perhaps being offered your ideal job.

_____

_____

_____

_____

8.   **Energy Projections:** Our personal energies are never contained. They affect everything—your moods, feelings, and emotions. Your energy projections allow you to create anything you so desire. As The True Source shared with me, "What You Think, You Create, and What You Create, You Experience!" You are all the energies created by your thoughts and your acknowledgment of those thoughts. Imagine your energy like a laser beam going right to that manifestation. It is like your eyes are wide open and you are visualizing the laser beam going to your manifestation and creating it now in your life. Below, describe how you will use the laser beam to create your manifestation.

_____

_____

_____

_____

9. **Imagination:** If you desire to manifest something in your life, you must add the thought to imagine that your dream (manifestation) is already here and you are living and experiencing, knowing and partaking in it. Think of it as being like a movie. You are the producer, the director, and the actor playing all the parts. It is important that you feel the emotion—the excitement and the joy—knowing full well that it is already in your reality. Describe below how you are going to do this and how it will feel.

_____

_____

_____

_____

10. **Acceptance:** Once you manifest something in your life, it is important to know you are worthy and that is already coming forth into your life. Acceptance and belief go hand-in-hand. Know that everything exists and is now open for you to experience. Nothing that you manifest positively in your life can be blocked unless you refuse to accept it. It is your doubt that slows down or blocks the acceptance. List below why you are worthy of accepting all of your positive manifestations.

_____

_____

_____

_____

11. **Trust:** You must have unyielding and unbending trust that you are worthy of your manifestation and that it will soon appear in your life for you to have the joy and

experience you have manifested. It is time for you to affirm and trust that it is now coming to you. It is best that you do not try to figure out how it's going to happen; just believe that it is going to happen. Think about a little child asking for their birthday or Christmas gift, knowing and trusting their Christmas gift or birthday gift will come forth in their life. List below your memories of times when you knew and trusted something would occur in your life and it did manifest.

_____

_____

_____

_____

12. **Affirmations:** Affirmations are certain thoughts (energy creations) that will assist you in bringing forth your manifestation. By expressing the affirmation, you come to realize, trust, and believe in your words and thoughts that are now coming forth to you. Affirmations combine vibrations, frequencies, energy projections, imagination, belief, acceptance, and trust. Think of it this way: If you go to a restaurant and you tell the waiter, "I want food," but you do not specify what you desire, nothing will be served to you or the food provided may not be to your liking. When manifesting, you do not need to go into huge detail. All you really need to do is express the manifestation using the word "perfect." What does that mean? It means everything your soul desires will bring you the unlimited joy and satisfaction that match exactly what you have been hoping for or something even better.

The word "perfect" means what you desire and more to complete your ideal manifestation. List below the perfect affirmations for your manifestation. An example would be: I desire that I am now manifesting my perfect car. This means everything I desire for a car and even more that will make me very happy.

_____

_____

_____

_____

It is advisable that you make a list of all your affirmations that have come to be true and the date when they happened. The reason to do so is that when you feel doubt, you can look at your list to see how successful you have been. If, however, your affirmation has not yet manifested, just realize you need to do it over again because you still feel doubt. Remember, you must be positive and that your soul will assist you in achieving your manifestation. Another reason you may not have manifested what you want yet is that your soul knows when the perfect timing for it will be and whether it will be correct for you or not. Sometimes your ego gets in the way in regards to what you think you want to manifest and the proposed manifestation is really not coming from your soul's urging. The best way to achieve this is to meditate to ensure what you want is a right action and a correct exchange and not solely to boost your ego or for some selfish reason.

I believe in you! Remember: "YOU ARE UNLIMITED!"™

What is Love?

Love is an extension of life, and life is an extension of love. The two are indistinguishable. Without love there is no life, without life there is no love. You must first learn to love yourself for what lies within you is the beauty of life. The two are intertwined and you must learn to nurture that seed of love within you. This can be compared to planting a seed into the ground. First, you must prepare the ground like you must prepare yourself to accept it. Then you fertilize it with caring, acceptance, and watering it with faith. As the seed of love begins to grow in your heart, you come to the realization it is life within you. Now the seed continues to grow into a stem and eventually becomes a flower. You begin to realize the flower must be nurtured with the sun, warm wind, and rain. As the plant blossoms and unfurls its petals, showing its beauty; you come to the understanding, like the flower, you are created out of love letting love bloom forth. Your essence is pure love. First, you must be in service to loving yourself in a kind and gentle way. The realization that on your journey of life, you need to take care of yourself by expressing acceptance, non- judgementalness, inner knowing, and eventually birthing forth into unconditional love

Love must be nurtured by faith, hope, and desire, to become an extension of love so others may feel it as well. It is not about the sacrifices you make in life; rather, the love you spread in life and in your spiritual work. Knowing full well whether it is accepted or not accepted, you are always doing right action and correct exchange with the expression of unconditional love.

The emotion of love comes from your essence, your beingness, understanding full well that you are created out of love, by love, with love, and from unconditional love. Once you have acknowledged this within yourself, then you are to share this with someone you deeply love and care for. Together, the two of you, are to spread the love throughout the universe. There is no forgiveness without love and there is no love without forgiveness. You must forgive yourself realizing that everything you have experienced is created out of love to understand what love is truly about. It is not about control, manipulation, fear, death, doubts, insecurities, or materiality; it is a fine silky texture of loving yourself, knowing full well it is necessary to embrace THE TRUE SOURCE'S UNCONDITIONAL LOVE. The reconnection with THE TRUE SOURCE'S UNCONDITIONAL LOVE can only exist by acknowledging this love within yourself. Love cannot be expressed with flowery words. Love is something that is felt deep within your soul and in your heart. Words express love, but the emotional energy of love is felt deep within you to remind you, that it is the glue that holds your body together in this universe. For you see, without love there is no life, without life there is no love. There is nothing but love. It is the only energy that exists in the now and forever. Love can never be extinguished, only set aside. Love commands that it be expressed in every way possible. Remember, YOU ARE LOVE, BECOME LOVE!

"YOU ARE UNLIMITED!" tm.

Dr. Michael Gross/T.S.

About the Author

Dr. Michael Gross is an author, professional keynote speaker, transformational coach, and entrepreneur. His past careers include marketing and sales, entrepreneurship, and being the CEO of several corporations. He has also been an instructor/professor at City University, Bellevue, Washington, where he taught courses in economics, marketing, and business communications. He has been retained by several international corporations as a consultant. He also has hosted a monthly international radio show.

Michael's wide range of interests have led him to acquiring many degrees and certifications. He has doctorates in energetic healing and psychology from American Reiki Institute and dual master and bachelor's degrees in human services and gerontology from New Hampshire College. He is also a graduate of the University of Washington's School of Certified Professional Guardianship and Tacoma Community College's School of Hypnotherapy. He is a certified reiki master healer teacher, a Roger Callahan trained thought field therapist/teacher, a King County Bar Association trained guardian ad litem, and a nondenominational minister.

For over a third of a century, Michael has been on a spiritual path as an intuitive, healer, spiritual counselor, transformational coach, and teacher. Through the guidance of spirit, Michael has assisted others in their personal quest for self-empowerment, helping them to create the lives they have long sought and bring forth their intuitive abilities. He has traveled to Australia, New Zealand, South America, the British West Indies, the Dutch Antilles, and across the United States teaching and lecturing on metaphysics, self-empowerment, and healing. Currently, he is a life coach and spiritual coach, a multidimensional healer, and a teacher of classes in spirituality, self-empowerment, reiki, and other modalities. His seminars have included soul retrieval, cellular release, prosperity, and mental-emotional-spiritual healing. Many of his current clients and students are third generation.

In concert with God, the True Source, Michael has achieved great success and miraculous healings. He employs the various healing techniques and tools that were given to him by God, the True Source. Michael works multidimensionally to achieve healing and balance in people's lives. With the assistance of God, the True Source, he works on the physical body, emotional body, mental body, spiritual body, soul, over-soul, vibrations, cellular energy, spiritual frequencies, body alignment chakras, polarities, body timing, and even more. His use of soul retrieval has been highly successful and has changed many people's lives.

Ultimately, Michael teaches inner guidance, which allows his clients to develop new self-awareness and self-empowerment. By practicing these teachings on a daily basis, his clients are able to work out their personal problems, overcome adversity, and achieve dream-fulfilling lives. He has been called a luminary and a teacher's teacher, but he remains humble, knowing the work he does all comes from God, the True Source.

ABOUT DR. MICHAEL GROSS'S SPIRITUAL COACHING AND HEALING

Dr. Michael Gross's mission is to help all those who desire to reconnect with God, the True Source. Once this is achieved, it will help other souls achieve their missions and goals to change the mass consciousness of this planet, bringing about enlightenment, love, joy, perfect health, prosperity, abundance and peace.

By working with Michael, you will experience your soul's vibration being raised as you reconnect with God, the True Source. Many gifts will also be given to you if you truly desire to bring about great and positive change in your life.

Each Tuesday evening at 6:30 PM Pacific Time/9:30 PM Eastern Time, Michael hosts a teleseminar series in which he is open to all questions and conversations concerning spirituality. To join this free teleseminar, simply call 202-926-1059 and enter access code 125446#. Michael will look forward to your participation and answering any questions you may have.

Also, on the second Saturday of each month at 6:30 PM Pacific Time/9:30 PM Eastern Time, Dr. Michael Gross hosts a "Mass Consciousness Planetary Healing" call using the same number above. Both of these calls are free and open to the public. To access all the replays of these calls, please visit www.DrMichaelGross.com

If you wish to pursue your relationship with Michael further, he is available for consultations, intuitive readings, spiritual seminars, healings, cellular release, past life regression, soul retrieval, and much, much more.

Please contact Michael for a complimentary, twenty-minute conversation about how he may help you.

253-859-5639 (office)
253-222-1096 (private cell)
drmichaelgross1@gmail.com
www.DrMichaelGross.com

ABOUT THE INTERNATIONAL INSTITUTE OF SELF-EMPOWERMENT

I would like to share some exciting news. Sometime during the year 2019, I received a spiritual message to form a nonprofit corporation. As of August 14, 2020, I received the official designation from the Internal Revenue Service fulfilling my dream. The International Institute of Self-Empowerment was officially designated a 501(c)(3) nonprofit corporation.

MISSION STATEMENT:

Creating self-empowerment opportunities to help individuals find Self-Worth, Self-Love, and Self-Esteem.

VISION STATEMENT:

To assist diverse beneficiaries in the personal quest for Self-Empowerment, helping them to create the lives they have long sought. As recipients of the organization's programs, they will learn to bring forth their innate intuitive abilities while developing into insightful community leaders. The goal is that, with the Institute's guidance, beneficiaries will raise their standards and enlighten the world, channeling their energy in a more positive direction.

Among the institute's many goals, we envision assisting victims of domestic violence and abuse. The statistics have shown that domestic violence is increasing, and The International Institute of Self–Empowerment will provide the resources to ensure those in need have safe shelters and assistance in seeking reentry into a healthy environment.

VALUE STATEMENT:

Core Values:
- Self-Worth, Self-Love, Self-Esteem

- Respect

- Confidence

- Direction in Life

- Compassion

- Empathy

- Security

- Community

- Personal accountability

- Financial Independence

SOLUTION:

The International Institute of Self-Empowerment will provide guidance and solutions to teach beneficiaries how to release unhealthy belief systems. In doing so, they will be able to recognize fears, doubts, blocks, anxiety, and feelings of victimization. By working with qualified coaches, the beneficiaries will improve their level of Self-Worth, Self-Love, and Self-Esteem, empowering them to create a more positive future.

I invite all of you to look at the website to further understand our mission and goals.

TheInternationalInstituteOfSelf-Empowerment.org

In order for us to facilitate the nonprofit's mission and goals, we are in the process of obtaining grants and open to receiving any tax-deductible donations. These donations may be sent to:

The International Institute of Self-Empowerment
8113 79th St. SW.
Lakewood, WA 98498

If you have any questions, feel free to call me at (253) 222-1096. Your participation and any suggestions or help you wish to provide is most appreciated.

Thank you,

Dr. Michael Gross
President, The International Institute of Self-Empowerment

BOOK DR. MICHAEL GROSS TO SPEAK AT YOUR NEXT EVENT

Choosing a professional speaker for your next event is easy. Look to Dr. Michael Gross to leave your audience members enlightened and ready to overcome their obstacles to accomplish their dreams. Whether your audience is 10 or 10,000, in North America or on any other continent, Michael can deliver a custom-designed message of inspiration and spiritual awakening at your next meeting or conference.

One of the most fascinating and spiritual speakers of our generation, Michael will entertain, inspire, and encourage your audience members to strengthen their connection with God, the True Source, and leave them ready to achieve a new spiritual level in their lives. By sharing personal stories, ancient wisdom, and God-given messages, Michael will leave your audience wanting more but also knowing how to achieve it.

Michael can speak to your group on such topics as:

- How to reconnect with God, the True Source
- How to work out karma and karmic debt

- How to heal your past so you can move forward

- Reincarnation and how to remember your past lives

- The Twelve Spiritual Laws to live by

- The Law of Attraction and how to manifest what you desire

- The Gift to Heal

- How to attract your made-in-heaven miracle mate

- Create prosperity and abundance now

- How to free yourself from the blocks in your life

It's unlikely you will ever hear such a humble, memorable, and engaging speaker as Michael Gross.

Contact Michael today for a complimentary, thirty-minute pre-speech interview so he can learn about your organization's needs and how he may help you.

253-859-5639 (office)
253-222-1096 (private cell)
drmichaelgross1@gmail.com
www.DrMichaelGross.com